Erstwhile Orbits & Newformed Spheres:
Collected Poems
By Umohowet Taushi Yelayu

Copyright © Umohowet Taushi Yelayu
Sumahrumet Entertainment
All Rights Reserved
Washington D.C.
Scotts Valley, California
Seattle, Washington
London, England, U.K.

No parts of this publication may be reproduced, stored in a retrieval system, or transmitted in any form or by any means, including electronic, mechanical, photocopying, recording, or otherwise, without the prior written permission of the copyright owner.

This is a work of nonfiction, based on real persons, places, and events which have been presented in a poetic interpretation and with poetic license. Names and identifying details have been changed to protect the privacy of individuals.

Table of Contents

2003: When First I Fell In Love 1
I. The First Mesa: The Contention of Conflict (Sep Tu'umo alp') 2
II. Your Palace In My Earth (Ge'ut kr'ah sem) 7
III. The Holiness of Consumption (Seh'Fipuh Womah) 9
IV. The First Earth (Huwarum'lep het) 11
V. Possible (Suhtom Eto'al'herut tep) 16
2004: When First I Knew A Thing Had Been Broken 18
VI. Chinatown (Suila Ke'wuayo Om) 19
VII. The Prophet's Spice Truck (Kuwualiyo 'Amo Arum Et) 25
VIII. New Mexico (Sa'hn ouno al) 34
IX. The Hajj of Adulation (Ko'qm Ano Et'ruim l) 38
X. Holy Oil (Joam'el nkt halum) 40
2005: When First I Was Off-Bearing & Confounded 41
XI. The Invention of Renunciation (Qaj huaml herau el) 42
XII. Insight (Perah'ehum amp'helet sumhp) 46
XIII. Hotels as Life (Se'to Tahum Wa'ho 'el) 50
2006: When First I Was Consumed With Disillsuion 52
XIV. Caliweto (Seh'um Ato hu'al) 53
XV. Amaretto (All The Reasons I Hate You) (Rikl'ewop Eruop) 57
XVI. Apocalypse (Haru'kla pu'sham'het) 59
XVII. Upside Down Rainbow (Gu'joap uro ruh nehl) 60
XVIII. Self Righteous (Far'uh leh'in to) 62
XIX. The Prophet's Renunciation - Spoken Word (Ruh ahu le'ain'mu) 70
2007: When First I Entered The Vast & Arid Wilderness 76
XX. The Naked God (Saro'howet Oma'leu peh) 77
XXI. I Am A Coward (Huj'om Wer'yup Kal'peh) 81

XXII. The Refusal of the Embryo (Fu'manh Het) 83
XXIII. Captor (Be'rahum pelao'tuom'h) 85
XXIV. For Certain (Wum'jahu oi'lum a'pi) 88
XXV. Rebel or Saviour (Sei'sa le'anutph ai'tuh) 96

2008: When First I Became Lost In The Mirages 100
XXVI. Kinetic Slavery: Love As Religion (Se'luwoh A'um Vl'eop) 101
XXVII. Suihallawuiyou (or The Girl At Ota'lu'kume) (A Vision) (Art Piece Representing Mental Breakdown and Recovery) 109

2009: When First I Found Water In The Desert 119
XXVIII. The Logistic of If/Then (Keta'sep l) 120
XXIX. I See Without Time (Si'lahu so'phet qua'heht) 125

2010: When First I Returned From My Pilgrimage 129
XXX. The Places I Know Of (Suma hotatu pawi umaro'met) 130
XXXI. The Transfiguration of Breath (Sa'atahlp Etahuamet Ka'Sephml O') 133

2012: Songs For A Defining Year Of My People & Generartion 139
XXXII. The Breakdown of Matter (Komo Ummaet L'kuawol) 140
XXXIII. Womyn's Sad Hymn Against Birth (Set'ku Pajhmu Karom'l) 144
XXXIV. Nebula Being (Sora Tui Teh'impko Wa'a O) 149

2013: When First I Rejoined My Old Tribe 154
XXXV. In-Formation (A'kamaulauah atamammah) 155
XXXVI. Predominate (Ahtahmah'eh Ra'al'maht'ma'al) 161
XXXVII. Streetlights – A Song of Sadness (Ket'emll a'wao lt) 171
XXXVIII. More Than This - A Song of Longing (A'tukuwo'ua'ah'ulaul Mmah'tah'to'weh'l) 173

2016: When First I Realized A Thing Had Been Broken Again 174
XXXIX. Pastel and Shell (Eck Hu'wotm Ki'amo'go) 175
XL. To Witness Totality (Ka'haroum Pa'Net Huam'l) 180
XLI. The Merkabah of Modernity (Et' Umlah Amah) 184

2018: When First I Walked The New Orbit 187
XLII. The Long-Haul of Survival (Ma'ashl m'ahluwal'ah puwo'ah) 188

XLIII. I Name Myself (Umatahmolo L'Yuehamolo) 192
XLIV. The New Orbit (Eh'to oh'lahw'h Mah'la) 194
Dedications 196
Author's Message 197
Review 199

Words that have no meaning, and are in no language, should be pronounced as they are; the word sounds transmit the emotion or energy intended.

An Invocation

"...and when we learned that we had been
revolving around worlds
that were barren, possessing no sustenance,
whose gravitational pull threatened to rip us apart,
trapping us in event horizon,
worlds that were noxious, damaging us cellularly,
to the signature of our self-construction,
to the atomic particles of our mortal-foundation...

We abandoned those orbits,
And there was wild roaming, and uncertainty,
In merciless cosmic wilderness,

But, there we realized a thing:
That we needn't orbit bodies no better than our own,
that we could build our own habitation
In the spacetime of life,
and, in it, come to knowledge,
And merely by acceptance of that knowledge
It was revealed to us,
that we are our own source and satellite,

And with this knowing,
We remade ourselves,
as all things first did by the desire to exist,
And we defined and rebuilt,
Until we were as we should be,
both source and satellite...

And there,
in that knowing and being,
in the state of consistent evolution,
we could sing of our erstwhile orbits
And the newformed spheres"

2003: When First I Fell In Love

I. The First Mesa: The Contention of Conflict (Sep Tu'umo alp')

If you wished it,
I'd proclaim the sky was whole made of chocolate,
Because you are golden eyes in rainbow country,
Sunlit, Sacrosanct, Your being is Love-Law,
I feed off the grain of your intimacies,
lost in the very fiber of your being,
the caverns and nuances of you,
I am a depleted world,
and you are the civilization,
Beloved to me are your eccentricities,

The strawberry wine, which we spiced with
nutmeg, glistens on your lips,

Boundless,
possessing no void and no empty,
But I am careful taking from your well,
Lest I deplete you as I have been depleted,

your beauty is hardly understood, even to me,
you walk into the room with the wind,
it is impossible to ignore you,
you pour love into the All around you,
how, then, can you not be loved back

Yet, your flaws are as awkward as your perfection,
you are quaint, inhuman
and I am at your mercy,
you don't think twice of me, you stamp upon me at
your will,
I am the slave to your master, and all that that
implies

You are a dark spot on the sun,
a hole in the ozone,
And our bruises matched in a way that made us
kindred beings,
a thread of peace extends from your consciousness
to mine,

Today,
the sky is undecided
as to opposition of the sun or submission to it,
so it preaches of revolution:
allowing some clouds in its dominion's protection
to mutiny against the sun's light,
and thus we plan for rainy days
simultaneously with a trip to the beach,
because we are unsure as in all things

our light causes the whole world
to seem psychedelic,

like how the sky is darkened during a nuclear

blast,
how everything is reduced to ash:
so too are our cares
drunk upon the hallucinogens of cacti water,
we find redemption, while lolling along
the inside of the garden,

in the hemisphere, the air from Italy has mingled
with Arabian spices,
and descends from the sky as a breeze,
like blackberries and dumplings,

newscasters speak on our transistor radio,
painting a picture of third world landfills,
populated by
tractors, cows,
and men, like midnight ravers,

today, as always, someone has to lose to broach the
chasm between us,
it's always me, you never do,

If only you'd take off your fear,
That shame & guilt, hurt & persecution,
lay them across the grass for just a second,
take off your ego like a well=worn-too-long jacket,
let a cold stone be your bed,
and a warm wind your cover,
maybe then you will know the paradigm you are,

I never intended to be trouble to you,
but I was under-prepared for all that you are,
I take these things so seriously,
and though I know it's never easy:

if you say you love me, I will believe you,
you don't have to mean it...

when first we were alone,
perhaps it was wrong to do what we did,
and perhaps that is why I was drawn to you
so deeply,
you pay me no attention,
but then our conversations write a complicated
and pointless song
which extends forever,
and sometimes I wonder if I have the energy to
write it over and over,

you sit across from me in the garden,
pretending that you have to leave shortly,

I know, as always, you want me to play the fool,
and ask, *Am I keeping you?*

Yes.

*Well, if so, then
can I keep you?*

This is the paradigm of us. We are civilization and paradise, but
We are Armageddon, and wastelands.

II. Your Palace In My Earth (Ge'ut kr'ah sem)

You...
play me, a game of cards,
I have become accustomed to your poker face,
just before you kiss me,

you behave like a child whose roll of the dice will
bring the win
and then you build your palace
in the country of my Earth,

You carry your burning sun to the blue & bulging-
cumulus-cloudy-sweet Dream Lodge of my sky
holding up a number globes to the Meta of my
person
You are mist,
the lord of the rock and water tempted lands,
you are the bold sea and warmed ocean tides,
the slow rise and fall of the old-surf,
you are the lord of error,
the harbinger of my amorousness,
and I release you at night only after we have
experienced greatest pleasure,
We are the Ego and the Vulnerability,
but you are the cause of my redemption,
the grace and salvation,
I pretend to be so strong,
aloof in my dependencies,

the Alpha male striding,
prideful in ultimate dominion,
but it as an honor to expose my vulnerabilities and
flaws to you,

You are the dawn and the dream,
and I am the drum which beats your arrival,

the atoms of several collective futures?
each one leads to us!

you peer into me like a witch doctor,
and redeem my heart,
your smile is the resurrection

of every love that is lost

III. The Holiness of Consumption (Seh'Fipuh Womah)

Nearly with tears in my eyes,
I begged for your being to contract like the fabric
of space upon me,
To bring you to the height of pleasure,
An unearthly psychosomatic caress,
From the body core to the extremities

Paradise came in the moments after,
When I buried my face in your shoulders,
And closed my eyes,
Consummation and consumption,

I wished for death-as-transformation within the
portal of your arms,
And you in mine,
Knowing that I could leave this world,
and that my life would have been complete for so
long
as I am locked into you,

I saw the universe as a mirror
and you as the reflection I've searched for

I have learned that
it's the moments after passion that are the soul-
mark of love

when the light from the afternoon sun is pouring
in the window,

and we are alone in a room,
disconnected from the rest of the Earth,
a bedroom as alternate dimension,

It's not the sex that heals me, instead
it's the moments after
when we are prepared to transform into
nothingness,
while we cling to each other,
when we hold so tightly that it seems we are
intentionally trying to crush our bodies and flesh
together
and meld into dust, energy, or a new being

It's the moment when I no longer care about
accomplishment, success, goals,
or the Earth,

When the pain of living and the joy of humanity is
forgotten,
when I want to transform into the elements of you
drifting into space

It's the space and time after orgasm
That define our love
And that heal me
When life has wounded and beaten me into
foldedness

IV. The First Earth (Huwarum'lep het)

You elude me in breezes that capture your fragrance
the way you walk to my door,
the wind brewing in your ears, a storm,
the sun shining in your jeweled pieces,
Is it possible that I could have been birthed from a place in your heart and never knew it?

When I don't know the words to say,
it is more than I have known,
As such, I am at your mercy,

There are things I only wished for
which you knew and made real,
dreams I did not yet see,
which you beheld and created,

When love is like this, it is greater than even life
I am your servant for as long as you will have me
I am at your mercy for as long as your mercy permits,

Daisies grow untended,
rife at the foot of a shack we once visited,
they were not there when first we came,
And you left me when they were still seedlings,
I know because we planted them,

A flooded marsh runs through fields we once trod,
it was not always so,
for when we trod those fields of corn,
under the shadows of wooded crosses,
that marsh was but a river that threatened to rise
come the rainy season

time, then, has elapsed since last we spoke,
time, then, has passed us by,
time, then is not on our side,

My face is aging, it seems,
Perhaps I get wiser,
the sky seems less and less the same shade of blue,
the trees no longer a vivid hue of green,
the field, once golden amaretto grain, is now black
soil and pebbles,

It feels like the whole Earth ages with me
But with you, I never feel weary,
when it is love like this, even life is less important

You see, I woke up at daybreak,
You woke up at dawn,
I endure the deep night and the high day, I thrive in the
amber moments,
You blossom in the hot heat of noon and the depth of
crescent moon hours,

But still you are oxygen
You are all that I have wept for
You give me courage to reveal the emotion we promised to hide

But there we fears,
I know because we spoke of them,
Could us together and our forever bear enmity,
might we be unable to coexist,
We feared this world,
That it might not allow us,

Did your fear of those unanswered questions,
Cause you to leave me in those fields,
That even as I travel the world apart from you,
I see glimpses of you in all things
Or,
Was your wish to leave uninfluenced by those fears,
Does your Earth spin elsewhere,

I would ask you, but I am sure
The reason is enshrouded in the venom of a cobra,
you can never get it, except by death,
for what it's worth,
Therefore only conjecture will do

But I'll wait for as long as you will have me wait

Because it is more than I imagined,
it is greater than life

And I am at your mercy
A su merced; what is your peace?

A waged war in the heart but not on soil soil?
Bent fingers mixing magic, planting seeds,
colors that bloom in summer,
petals frilly and large, stem running deep

Fragility is the wish of the broken,
who have been through storms and giants,
Frosted hearts, my dreams splashed at your feet
like hot coal,
wishes under your hammer like nails,
life in your words like a soft killing,
You tread harshly upon your enemies,
but tread lightly, please, tread carefully,
tread peacefully on this linen ribbon,
For it is fragile,
Like floating in space, wondrous,
cried laughter flying from the mouth,
few can begin to comprehend this magic,
a burst of flowers from a sun colored pupil,
flashing purple in the
reds,

dusking sky and setting sun,
gold dust on the prairie,
Magician whispers, love-rinsed daisies,
an ear of my design,
a flower forever stuck,
A rose that dares not grow,
Oh, yes, such magic,
loved, kissed, broken,
surrendered sunflower dreams,

A su merced; what is your peace,
Because I am at your mercy,

And if all this I can give you in word,
imagine what I can give you in life
When it is more than I imagined,
it is greater even than life
this is what I call you

You are the first earth

V. Possible (Suhtom Eto'al'herut tep)

I cannot think it possible for anyone to love you more than me,
you are the sea of comfort in an uncertain modern world
I trust that you are everything,
Summer or the snowy season,
We'll come back together,
I'm willing to wager that you can't sleep without me,
I can't find the air to breathe unless you show me to it,
Perhaps we should wager your heart for my soul and see if they are interchangeable
perhaps we should wager your future for my past, and forge both anew together,
my love is splashed unto your consciousness,
it may go as far as the eye can see,
my passion is what fuels the light around us,
it is inexhaustible,

you are the moment when grey clouds part just once to reveal blue sky,
a transcendent revelation

you are the moment between the end of the ringing of chimes,

and the beginning of the silence that follows,
the harmony of two opposites blended into that
space between,
individual but together as one,

Perhaps we should wager your life for mine
since they are one, what could we lose?

You are incense rising from an altar,
you are the candle which burns at night
you are the boatman at the river styx,
you guide me to judgement,

Perhaps we should wager you for me
we then would realize there is no separation,

Science should study your mystery

2004: When First I Knew A Thing Had Been Broken

VI. Chinatown (Suila Ke'wuayo Om)

I. 2003
We'll get no younger,
and wishing cannot make it so,
eternal sunshine: I am halfway between loving you
and leaving you behind,
the soul's atrophy, prayers unanswered,
wishes resigned to apathy,
reflecting your being,

paysage:
In an empty cafeteria,
three stories above the ground level,
the landscape of the city is spread before me
facing west,
like a painting through a window,
I peer across the miles
wondering what life might be where the horizon
curves

on a whim I went to Chinatown today
with **name removed**
we skipped school two hours before noon,

he and I spent hours breakdancing in front of an
elementary school
while the students looked out, their eyes alight,
yelling out the window

We were their bridge to paradise
for just one moment
between math and spelling lessons,

We carried our act to a park and a crowd gathered
around us, cheering,
name removed, of course, got most of the attention,
he is the confident one, I am not
but now I am used to surrendering to his
dominance,
the amour and the paramour of all people and all
things
that he receives,
I am pleased with the leftovers,
as he usually discards much

he was turquoise and I was jade,
I was Marlon and he was Shawn,
we were orange peels and liquor,

Nomad wanderers, we roamed,
The sun and sky was ours and the whole planet
belonged to us,
We are not wealthy though:
The journey is all we have

name removed joined the two of us as we
explored,
We settled at a garden park,

Near the river

laid next to the bridge
the one that gave us calm and enlightenment,

it begged us to remember ages when it was young,
instead of the rusted metal beams it had become,
pulley wheels as big as a building,
cords as thick as ten men,
and an abandoned watch tower atop it

We could see a wall of gentle rain
coming toward us
But we stayed there
And when it came we hid under the temple gate,
until the rain was gone, leaving behind colossus
clouds,

we watched the sun set, standing there,
the whole world was bathed
in amber, blood, and sunflower,
the colors of the setting sun,
evanescently manifesting in transience,

when the solar disc had disappeared on the
horizon,
avoiding the moon, as it always does
We walked across a field that led to a different
bridge,

The train bridge where many rails met,
The one that transformed us
The seed bridge...

The cement balances that caused the bridge to rise
and fall
were as massive as consequence,
Held in place by thick cords and suspended in air:
they looked like commandment tablets descending
from the heavens
We posed for pictures on the bridge,
To put them on the internet so we could
Impress our friends,
Then followed the rails further down,
We were fearless, kings,
The railroad our dominion
Staring at the rail tracks as they continued forever
west,
Into the vibrant colors left behind by the setting
sun,

In that moment, we were telepathic, a shared
thought:
If we could walk those rails as far as they went,
and leave everything behind
We would have
No matter how far west they went,
Whether California or over the horizon curve on
an angle into the sun

We would have gone, and been consumed,
By California, or the sun,
But we were not strong enough for the journey
And we had dedicated so much of our lives to the others in our lives
Even before we knew what that would cost

On the train ride back, we sat silently,
Staring out the window, with our headphones on,
Empty but for the experiences we created,
Wandering nomads,
We had no past and no future,
We lived for the now,
The past struck us too deeply,
The future was blind water
What was behind stabbed violently at us,
and what is before us eludes us,

All we had was now, this moment,
Fearless because the only way we could live was to cling wildly and live desperately in this space

A voice in my head whispered silently,
"You haven't been happy in years..."

I'll get no younger, and wishing cannot make it so, eternal sunshine: I am halfway between loving you and leaving you behind, the soul's atrophy, prayers unanswered,

wishes resigned to apathy,
reflecting your being

VII. The Prophet's Spice Truck (Kuwualiyo 'Amo Arum Et)

Jamaica, January 21, 2002
So psychedelic,
he makes the 60's seem tame,
such a saving grace,
he'd make Jesus do a double take,
he left me a haiku
wrapped around one of the milk bottles,
on my porch

I.
drink this slow made brew
it blends death and embryos
your fortune chooses

I knew
he would be out
by the chasm,
his truck with one wheel dangling over the ledge,
to tempt fate,
gathering shells and spices near the shore,
for the poisons and potents he made
while his sweetheart lady strummed an out of tune
guitar
I ran to find them
nearly dropping the milk bottles,
but encountered her along the way,

the guitar around her shoulders by the strap,
running along-side me to get to him,

we saw him
riding away on a banana boat,
towards one of the islands,
he waved at us mischievously,
as the boat rippled the still surface of the water,
like skin when one is pinched,
or bed sheets after making love,
or the sand when one drives a scythe through it to
find a water hole,

on the beach we found two pieces of paper, under
a rock
our names were on them, I read mine

II.
there is no such thing
as a scripture or the earth
you make religion

I knew I was not to share it with her
and turning to her she quickly hid hers,
her smile was four mischievous children
and mine was their prank,
we left the milk bottle and the guitar on the sand,
and swam after him for what seemed like hours,

in the water, we found a large floating bottle,
corked tightly, for us
inside: a dead butterfly and a live one,
a tiny capsule of oils containing shredded flowers
and spices,
a small piece of meat,
a note,
and a rose dipped in fragrant sunflower oil,
I took out the note,
she and I read it together,

III.
where the journey leads
incense, tulip, and ginger
the path is reward

the live butterfly inside flew away
we knew instantly what he meant
and continued swimming,
she pulled out two of the tablets he made for us,
wet with water now,
of cinnamon, amaretto, and ginseng,
shredded roses and mango,
and we ate them
a potent for energy,
it was abuse to make us swim after him to the
island
but we would do anything, for even the scent of
his breath,

so we swam harder, determined

the island was no wider than a living room
or a hut,
there were two palm trees and shrubs and the sun
was near setting,
he was there standing by a lemon tree, he snatched
one down,
then ripped a feather from a compliant bird
nearby,
he dipped the feather's tip into the water, to clean
it
she ravenously ripped open the lemon with her
teeth,
and squeezed it's juice into my cupped hands
I cupped as much as I could
and he dipped the feather into it,
and on a small piece of paper from his pocket,
he wrote quickly dipping the feather tip
into the cupped juice in my hand,
writing each letter carefully,
my hands could barely contain the juice
and twice she ripped open a new lemon
and squeezed it into my hand as a container,
as he dipped the feather tip into my natural ink
well,
writing a new note for us,
occasionally looking up at us smiling,
and we, giddy,

portion removed

the sun set as we
ravaged,

portion removed

shortly after he swam away *portion removed*
and she and I were left, alone on the island
we wondered at the purpose of it,
carefully she gathered shrubs and I took out my
lighter,
setting them ablaze,
night had come
we held the paper over the fire
and slowly the lemon juice materialized into a
readable color,

IV.
berate yourself well
I abuse and you receive,
is this the good life

his question was a barb to us and to himself,
even he knew, wavering back and forth
between master and friend, dominant to
submissive
and we both were ashamed,

we swam back to the main shore
by the glow of the moon and the plankton
and there he awaited, on the beach, several bon
fires lit around
his spice truck,
and a group of hippies who loved him, his
sycophants,
jammed to Dylan, Marley, and Apple,
he was inside,
shaman mystic man

a poisoned dart flew at my head,
I barely ducked, as it whizzed by, landing in the
sand
a note was attached to it,
I ran to read it

V.
how easy it is
to kill or to be killed,
we dodge sun and moon

a congratulation of my physical prowess,
and a contemplation of life
he was always testing,

we'd left the milk bottles on the beach,
when we swam out to meet him on the island
and now,

the bottles were tied to a log jutting out of the cold
waters,
his helper J****** must have seen us jump in,
and done it, knowing he would be rewarded,
she and I both stared at the helper, leaning against
the truck,
he was not as close to the prophet as we were,
but jealousy existed,
and the helper knew, and he loved it,

we walked over to the spice truck,
the prophet gave her a ring to replace the old one,
which he no longer cared for,
and me, a new guitar
the three of us sat, and he spoke

VI.
balance essential
sunflowers and morning frost,
the stasis of life

he pointed to a container of handmade ice cream
watching, he poured in cinnamon from his spice
truck
and the three of us ate out of it,
I reached in to get another spice for the goose his
hippies were cooking up
and found a note

VII.
teaching you is like
a turtle showing sparrows
how to fly the skies

he looked at us and spoke,
"Why?"

We could read his mind:
We will outgrow this, he meant,
one day, regular jobs await,
We cannot be free forever in a world of captivity,

I stared at the moon and responded,
Because I am tired of teaching revolution, and wisdom,
I am become a coward,
and for the time it is comfortable to be the subservient one,
if even to a lesser one,
he stared and nodded,
she sat next to me and strummed her guitar,
I contained my weeping

Two Haiku for Parting

Paris, March 30, 2005
I am wondering

if perhaps we have outgrown
the need for this life

Chicago, September 20, 2006
I do not think that
this can last much longer or
be what teaching is

VIII. New Mexico (Sa'hn ouno al)

Century broken by hand,
there's no easy way to drink bitter tears,
the gone around,
the worn down trail
The new feet,
And the water marked star,
There's no quiet way to maturity,
common knowledge:
we judge beings by sight, and hearts by mind
disconnected,
there's no stolen trail to dance around life,

The truth is
one day someone will know all the things Mama
never knew
anyone would know of you,
what we most fear is not the end of the age,
but giving every atom of our being to another
some masks are welded to the skin
some secrets are seared into the stuff of our soul

in this life, every being whispers a remote hope
and it flies,
sun-engulfing,
spiced with ecstasy
like half of creation,
defying logic and theory

like the golden dawn-light that breaks the night,
candle and river water,
It is our wish that these hopes reach the ear of fate
But in the rat race, the course of humankind is
toward the flame of the sun,
ever rising, we reach fate before our hopes do,

breakthroughs gained create more questions
of science and future
many saved,
many more killed,

greed and hate dance a dance that makes
promiscuous sex look like a sermon

Icarus syndrome defines humankind

The real truth is simple:
if we are but dust in the storm
than all our works can be nothing more
and if intellectuals do not heed a God,
then they would not fear unanswered questions
so afraid that one day they will reach the question
that cannot be answered,
and all their theory was in vain,
sad sad man,
century broken by hand

II.

Primitive man
Bones and beads
And wispy references
I compare it all to water, evanescently
transcendent, and rife,
blurred New Mexican street corners full of
bones and beads and wispy references
under sandy walkways and lifeless streets,
distorted from the tears that caress my face in salt
water
I am the ocean rising now, I think

I compare you to dreams of Desert plains,
and mother's favorite soap,
skies that speak of civilization,
the quintessential delusion of barbarian
humankind,
they describe eternity
Humankind's Endless movement forward,
the kinetic churning, the mechanic energy
the tenement hallways and blood stained porches,

Court jester politicked by the Hand of Fortune,
a word which still makes me tremble
uncomfortably,

Logically, could it be as simple as Whim and
Chance,

Existence is an orgasm,
a dream, a fight, or plain indifference,

Recycled ancient matter, we are so old,
But I take youth by absorbing:
I will not be forgotten by the numbers of history,

Rumi's field,
Blake's island in the moon

A mystic came yesterday,
seeking to resurrect,
but my favorite show was on, missed miracles,
his disciples told me his destination,
If we leave now, we may just catch him

IX. The Hajj of Adulation (Ko'qm Ano Et'ruim l)

Embryo, shell and life,
A path from realm to realm,
The bridge as cocoon and soil, during the hajj of adulation,
Seed transformed, enveloped in the pilgrimage of wind,
For spirits like outs, freedom is consumption,
transportation on beans of sun

We were an alternate dimension,
The whole world was out of color,
Two dimensions mixed, one timeline,
I'm still not sure how much was real, but you marked me,
Charcoal, ink, soul, consciousness

Splenetic

How many flights must I take to get away from you and all the spurs you stuck firmly in my flesh, piercing,
Wounds that reach to the soul
You planted enmity in me that took years to remove

Where the separatist journey first began,
It was here that we left it all behind,
New country,
Rainbow and soil,

The new satellite

I can't see the city because rebirth is blinding
I spend each moment focused on the sky
The light is a language I wish to decipher

Two branches from the same trunk
Two paths from the same root
Ice river, mountain sun,
In the space between, in the division, there is solitude

X. Holy Oil (Joam'el nkt halum)

When we first moved in,
my aunt said we needed to anoint
every room of the house with blessed oils
to cast out any dark spirits
left behind by the previous family,
or spirits that have occupied the space while it
was empty
awarded permission to remain by existing
within the sacred mark of four walls & roof

but what good would this spiritual balm do
against the demons we brought with us

the dark spirits that traveled with us

They have bathed in this oil before,
They know its ingredients,
They have mimicked it with their own,

They imitate us as we pray over the oil & bless it,
the incantation ingrained in their memory

What good is our oil,
against them...

: When First I Was Off-Bearing & Confused

XI. The Invention of Renunciation (Qaj huaml herau el)

Love has broken beyond repair,
and so we have vowed to kill it,
we are its destroyers

the double invention of carrying on,
the singular forgetfulness of compassion,
the last bolero of the night is always the saddest

You are a slit wrist,
you bring pain, yet you are self-inflicted,
memories progress even to the farthest reaches of
my mind,
where I do not want you present,
you are mere lustfulness,
You are not what I want,
and are nothing like what I need,

I don't want you around,

yet each time I invite you in with incensed
caresses,
and whispered melodramatics,
against a backdrop of blue,
and blues vinyls,
cracked and rugged
like my conviction against you

I despise your scent, but I inhale it each time,
and I wonder, is it simply because you are the love
I have been lacking,
is it because you are the sentimentality that I
eschew,
it is because you are the thing that I would desire,
were it not you,

my thoughts are divided
the central core of what we are is forbidden,
fission
you are nuclear

I give in because I have to, not because I want to,
and we go for seasons without a simple glance, or
an even touch,
I am without the strength to refuse you,
for I love what you contain,
Near me, you are innocent, brought down to the
level of a child,
it disfigures you, to see you in such openness,
it discomforts me to have you caress me,

I am uncomfortable in your presence,
You demand my gates be open,
you command my guard to be dismissed,
furious eyes, elusive speech, and higher vibrations,
letting you in makes me feel unwholesome,

I should be a stone wall, protected against all souls
and matter

uncanny, obtrusive,
unearthly
a red moon,
solar eclipse,

you are like standing next to one of those giant
electric windmills, with no fear,
like looking into the face of God while holding
hands with the Enemy,

it is unusual to allow you into such hallowed
space,
I know once you are in my Mind-Place,
you will hurt me by the very nature of what we
are,

this is the command you have,
you weaken my defense,
havoc within,
and then you repair me,
cyclic, I see you, leave you,
and despise you, need you,
you should be cursed,
you should be damned,
for you have corrupted me,

Jazz in the background,

The last note from the jukebox,
the sound of the final bell at the bar,
when everyone is headed home,
As the sun slowly rises, more depressed than we are,

when the trumpets play their last bolero,
this is the saddest song ever known,

you are each space between the letter of each lyric
and I am each chord, and the melody...

XII. Insight (Perah'ehum amp'helet sumhp)

You are not aware of how well I see you,
You look different, somehow, something's
changed, something inside,
Something deep inside that I cannot guess or
procure,
but simply: I know it in my heart,
Something has changed, perhaps your eyes or your
nose,
your smile or your soul

Yes, your soul has changed, or perhaps mine,
your intimate soul, or perhaps mine

You wear new veils, new styles, new clothes,
new beliefs, new life

you have matured
As have I,

you speak so highly of me,
so beautifully...

Don't think of me so religiously, though
I still fear that I can hurt you,
I still have my flaws, untended and not yet mended

What if I said I never really knew you?

What if I said that I didn't really trust you?
What if I said that after all these years, I only loved you for who you
were because you always tried to love me for who I was?

But in reality,
I only loved who you were,
I never loved you for who you've become

Don't think of me so religiously

I only love the way that
I love the way
you love me

Which simply means that I might just like the feeling

The feeling of loving, the feeling of being loved

But what if I don't really love you?

Don't hold me in such high esteem,
I never trusted you,
I couldn't see through the shell you possess,
I couldn't know the real you
I didn't know where to go, who to trust, what to do

I didn't know what the future held
I didn't know what to believe, and I didn't want to
pretend anymore
And so in complacence I chose you,
But I couldn't see through it

Don't think of me so religiously,
We are still accountable for everything we've
done,
But if every rose and midnight kiss was just done
for the comfort,
What if I only loved you for the comfort?

Don't think of me so religiously
You became the leader of my life,
You become the dictator in my country of loving
eyes and
whispered dreams,
But even when you became the chief of my desires,
I couldn't see through them...

Purity cleans the cesspool
And now I see through the veils on your body
Every sensuous curve is a valley of lies
Every time we made love, I wondered why,

I see through you,

through what we were,
through what we have become,
Is it possible that this was never love?

Don't think of me so religiously,
I have my flaws. not yet mended,
I still can hurt you,
I might never have loved you,
what if it all was empty desire, the want for comfort,
the need for love, the fantasy of family, the slavery and captivity
of your dominating love

Don't think of me so religiously
I can see through...

XIII. Hotels as Life (Se'to Tahum Wa'ho 'el)

The year I lost the competition,
we stayed in a hotel in South Beach
the concierge attached us to the Fourteenth Floor

On the elevator, we noticed there was no button
for the Thirteenth Floor,

The elevator operator regaled us with a tale,

"In the old days, hotels avoided having a
Thirteenth Floor,
Because it was considered bad luck"

I asked,
"...but isn't the Fourteenth Floor
technically the Thirteenth Floor since they just
skipped it..."

The elevator operator responded,
"...technically..."

We remained silent,
I was uneasy the whole time we stayed there,
because
the analogy felt like life as I had come to know it

Labeling a bad thing as good
doesn't change its nature

Denying the sadness doesn't deliver us from it

Blocking out the pain
doesn't erase it...not for long,

Maybe we should call it what it is,
and take away the superstition
which invites our fears to us

Maybe we should live,
in the dichotomy

2006: When First I Was Consumed With Disillusion

XIV. Caliweto (Seh'um Ato hu'al)

I. Prelude

Like a pendulum in the mist,
your heart still beats life rhythm,
though I can't see it,
Chicken heads and goat blood stain the streets of utopia,
and an old whore sells spice,
in the City of Heaven, the place of man's broken gods
I thought I saw you in spilt blood yesterday,
as the world around me spun into colorful lights and
distant faces dripping the liquid of roots and tonic,
Dancers wrapped in foil, feathers, and sex grind organically
in the night,
And the tap of shoes upon the concrete
dream up a song that deny this empty existence,
They're selling spirits in the bar and
Once again, we have to choose again between God and
liquor,
the spirits and the Spirit,
But the bar is closer than the cathedral...
confused revelry
Here in the utopia you left me,
This city is unstoppable, the army in the
possession of the lecherous,
Brown paper bags disguise paradise,

I came back here only to see if anything ever changed,
But I lost my passport and my ticket,
Grinding passionately with four hundred lovers

Orgies are law

II. Reality
When did we succumb to complacence?
Sunsets bathe the city in spiced orange,
the elevator train rushes by,
highrise apartment
Western grapefruit sun,
passengers staring at me as I stand on the balcony,
They think I am appreciating the masterpiece,
orbit, star and atmosphere,
But it's the last thing on my mind,
They say I'll need two pills a day to be normal,
It wasn't always like this,
Tea in my cup,
Consciousness burning my soul
The sounds of the city up too loud
I'm down too much,
Prodigal son,
Nowhere job,
Sadness is the byword,
My playlist full of the quiet songs,
Everyone who sees me must think I'm happy
But the passengers on the train: their sad eyes:
It is only those eyes that are real

III. Realization

It dawned on me,
that I had been living for nothing,
from each exciting moment to the next,
with dull spaces of melancholy and nostalgia in between,
it dawned on me that everyone who was old was older,
and I was getting no younger,
it dawned on me that even without rose colored glasses,
it was still simpler then,
because then,
I worried over busy streets and neighborhood bullies,
now my worries are titanic,
they wish for wisdom, but it oh so very depressing to understand the world around you without the foolishness of youthful folly,
This is a carnival, if you could pull me so deep
I would never want to leave,
Someone, touch my back and tell me if my wings are still there,
or have I lost them to the serpent's apple,
...and how can I get them back?
This is a festival, we don't listen to the wise,
we don't obey the prudent, only the wild sing our song,

and only we sing the truth,
Sing and laugh, you also
We shall live to be old
I hear the soaring of the phoenix,
the seraphim high above,
lumineux,
A cursed palace of rubble and emptiness,
Trifle to feud to war,
War to slaughter and holocaust,
Show me a quiet way around the sunset
So this day goes on,
Prove that we are more than uncried tears
summer's grace, bring light.
Burned tragedies,
Lover's night,
Raise the sweet day again
before it is usurped by the pain of all that has been,
Show me a quiet way around the sunset,
Once where she will not despise if I refuse her

XV. Amaretto (All The Reasons I Hate You)
(Rikl'ewop Eruop)

You are liquor,
birther of mystery, bountiful dream-worker,
entrancing destroyer,
sweet, organic,
drunk from your taste
I forget you are poison,
you are a kind death,
your lips are flowers floating in liquid,
your taste, I compare to salt water and saltier skin,
the taste of sex, I call you bountiful,
your hair is as a grassland,
unkempt but full of arrogant lilacs,
narcissistic demands,
you are ancient as stone and tidal waves,
the first destruction of man,
the city beyond the horizon in the sky of life,
the city of God beyond the veil of Eden,
the place of death where no one will go,
where the sun does not shine but once,
where the moon does not go but twice,
where the stars do not consider,
you are the fool's ransom,
You call sailors to wreck with a siren song,
You are a hymn to child sacrifice,
you build the curriculum of social suffering,

Cultural stigma, the evil intelligence,
I call you lust, for you always smell of days-old passion,
fleeting touches, disaster, and soap,
those who dream of you are lost, amidst fancies and unmentionable thoughts,
forgotten in the sand of unrighteousness,
floating through the lair of the heart,
you invoke the nature of time, place, and being,
you are word, sound, and logic,
boastful death in every whisper-touch
you are the paradox, the questions around the nature of rising smoke,
nightmares tremble from the mystery of your thought,
your lyric is an invocation,
those who are lost come to you not because they desire you,
but because they don't wish to continue on,
usurped by the slavery of dominion,
You make the heart weary
The first palace and last outlaw are lost in your tangle

XVI. Apocalypse (Haru'kla pu'sham'het)

You always tell me to look down while I climb,
hoping I will fall back into you,

Staring toward the horizon,
the orange suckled orb moans as it lowers over
baked land,
and treads water
as if exhausted

You ask
"Who taught you flight?"

Your fingerprints are on my shattered soul,
Your blood is on my broken wings,

I must mean the world to you,
For you to seek to destroy me so often

Wounded pets need no cage

XVII. Upside Down Rainbow (Gu'joap uro ruh nehl)

Your finger tips are acid,
daggers punch from your eyes, staring,
don't touch me

they say I'm crazy

today
before I jumped in the water, as it rained,
I noticed a rainbow,
and looking down I saw it's reflection in the water,
reflets dan l'eau,
reversed, inverted,
an upside down rainbow,
disturbed only by the exploding circles
the remaining rain made as it fell into the bay

when I jumped in I swam through as it rained,
and looked up to see the rainbow,
now constantly mutilated by the pelting drops of
water,
distorting the clear surface,
even in Neptune's dimension
looking up is still looking up,
happiness too,
is only a mirror reflection,
of the sadness we effervescently wear

swimming,
I become the shark that I am,
we are both cyanide, and ether,
look in the mirror of my eyes,
see the reflection of us

we do not belong together,
don't offer me your lust,
Happiness is like Juliet,
and I am Romeo awakening from the apothecary
to find her gone,
should I complete the tale,
modernized,
it would be so tragic,
I would miss my favorite shows composing it,
and you are not worth it

don't touch me,
your finger tips are acid,
daggers punch from your eyes, staring

we do not belong together

XVIII. Self Righteous (Far'uh leh'in to)

A butterfly kissed me on the cheek with his wings
after flying forth from a rosebush in my front yard
that I never cared for...

I. September 18, 2004, Chicago
Guru,
I am sitting outside of my mentor's house,
watching the white moon through pine trees turn
the sky into turquoise,
on a suburban block that looks entirely like the
street I once lived on,
a perverse side of me wonders what is happening
in the rooms of each house,
who is praying to God under the moon, do you
find me religious?
who is dreaming of a new satisfying life, do you
find me revolutionary or imperious,
like selflessness or honesty?
who is searching dusty books for a topical healing,
do you find me ironic or satirical, perhaps
sarcastic?
who is addicted to the latest craze,
do you find me voyeuristic?

who is making love, passionately like new love,
or sedately like married with four children,

do you find me orgasmic?
who is slowly dying,
do you find me morbid?
who is quickly living,
do you find me curious?
who is lying life,
do you find me spiritual?
who is living truth,
do you find me philosophical?

I have wondered if it turns me on to watch,
life and living
and to understand them by observation
even as they cannot see me,
to study them under the guise of love,
those closest to me, don't realize how calculating I
can be
and I have finally wondered,
if I ever knew real joy, or just the imitation of it,
will I ever learn authentic joy, did I ever know it?
dearest teacher, how many of my relationships
were based on lies and convenience,
do you find me perverse,
perhaps sadistic
I don't wish to be misunderstood,
or to misunderstand myself
I have discovered that dysfunctional people can
only love the way they are,

I am not so prideful to think myself beyond analyzation,
If I were to accept the conclusion that I am great,
does that make things any less difficult,
is a prophet ever welcome in his own homeland,
or a genius ever understood for the line he stands on,
the balance of dark and morning,
insanity and knowledge,
Do you find it self righteous,
that I no longer repress

II. August 14, 2005, Tokyo
Guru,
I had been searching
through means I had not yet understood,
I am just now beginning to understand:
They held me captive, but they were all so inferior,
and I no longer count it arrogance to admit this,
it is common knowledge,
I miss your light, promise me you'll right back in time,
and I will write you,
I am hesitant to even look into their eyes,
lest they see into my soul,
or I into theirs,
I have realized that I am pained,
because I am still healing,

if we must lose it all, or even if we must die, then
so be it,
but I am changing everything,
because I realize now,
we have been breaking all the rules

III. September 19, 2006, Cairo and San Francisco
Guru,
you bedeck me with an industrial bridge in front
of the sunset,
in Chinatown,
you entrance me with third world countries,
landfills,
and cows amidst heaps of trash,
depleted but spiritually strong

you enchant me with the promise of English
summers,
I have been waiting for a letter from you for so
long,
usually the wait is not this long when you travel,
you must have gone to the moon and back by now,
promise me we'll go to the moon,
before we part

I have realized now why you have become so
distant,

it was a lesson:
I was too dependent on you, too needy,
too dysfunctional, too foolish and headstrong, too unwise,
and now I am surpassing even you
and our dynamics have changed,
so I must not be dependent on you for knowledge and guidance,
but myself and my Creator,
yet I promise:
none of them love you or understand you as deeply as I do,
though our connection is broken

please do not weep, you were made for me and I for you,
do not find that erotic,
for we too many times confuse love with lust,
it is possible that you are my soul-mate,
but of kindred-ship, not of romanticism, so even though we part,
we will meet in a capsule of authority

so much like my childhood, I was always so repressed,
so imaginative, I had a fortune in my books,
and a treasure in my words,
I was never justified by them, I loved,
but I was never understood,

this was the rift I faced each time,
you were the only one who never knew that rift,

IV. August 18, 2007 - September 17, 2007 (edited after learning), Amsterdam
Guru, this will be our last correspondence,
please write back, as that will be the seal, the oath,
A butterfly kissed me on the cheek with his wings,
after flying forth out of a rosebush in my front yard,
that I hardly ever cut,
if I had known he would be there one day,
I would have trimmed it
more often,
you know what that means:
that I have finally found peace

V. undated, Hong Kong
Guru, I fear for you.
Time is against us. Time of the other history.
And the history of another place.
Time is against us, I say.
Promise me you will let me know you are well.
I am beginning to see you in the face of every one I encounter.
So unless you have mastered the ability to traverse plains spiritually,
then I am in such need of you that my mind plays me the fool.

Please inform me of your whereabouts.
I am not being clingy. But I am worried.

VI. September 27, 2008, Paris
Guru,
Where are you, I'm always writing to you with nor response.
And I've been crying since the summer.
We have become an old movie, a sweet autumn tale.
Perhaps if I pray to the fates and the stars, maybe you will return to me.

VII. July 12, 2009, Chicago
Guru
I know I promised I could live without you,
but it was a lie, please count it all self-righteous.
Return to me. I am lost without you.
See I am back in Chicago,
I returned to the place where we began,
The place we begun to part.
I had the best of intentions when we first met,
but you go where I won't, and you want what I don't.
Please don't make me choose between loneliness and you.
I'd sell my soul for your return, I cannot win.
I compare you to New Mexico, desert, bones, and spirituality,

you are everything to me.
I know I promised I could live without you,
but it was a lie, please count it all self-righteous

XIX. The Prophet's Renunciation - Spoken Word
(Ruh ahu le'ain'mu)

If no one speaks the
truth
who will teach the
crew
of sheep in blind pastures,
tree and
roots,
corrupt pastors
who can handle truth in a land of
bastard ways,
I'm
past the days
I spent mastering foreign
tongues,
I poured my soul and
lungs
into pleasing
infidels,
no triumphant
yells,
Living life in the day of
hell,
a whole life as propaganda,
lies light up and burn like a roman candle,
whose turn to take the mantle of
death,
what scandal is
left,

when all of life is based on a lie,
what scandalous
depth
will follow this rapturous
mess,
some consider it beauty to rape
gracefully
everything they face
inevitably
destroying land, space, and
sea,
I've never seen such
complacency,
Some run from truth, but the truth is facing
me,
the truth replacing the old
me,
I'm tired of chasing after gold
things,
false idols and old
dreams,
what untold means would
scold me,
enfold me,
you told me you're
holy
but there's holes in your
story,
why have I placed pain on a pedestal,
this earthy fetish
told

me it's only
goal
was to see the death of me,
hail to the chief, beautiful spacious skies,
amidst the amber waves of
grain,
and stories that a Lamb was
slain,
we invite the
pain and bite our tongue when the
rain comes,
a world full of Judas's paying the
same sum,
to betray a
Christ,
is it worth your
life,
thirty pieces of gold
the worlds a stage, will you take the
mask off,
a world of fakes, will the trumpets
blast off,
Zion even by mathematics measure all
righteous ability, pious acrobatics in the tongue of
probability,
athletic is the fight against
enemies,
the Lion is conquering all religious
mockery starting from topically based
inwardly
to optically placed,

I thought they said that they would
serve and protect,
rather
unnerve and neglect,
I'm nervous
as they say we worthless,
we're better off dead than believing common
reasons
that our
season
for freedom has ended,
where are my rights preacher,
you're speaking for the dead,
crooked balance in your hand,
got the
white collar on, but no
collar bone,
what does it cost us,
when religion is perverted into
lie after lie,
is it a
sign of the times?

Revolution is bred,
each time the worldplace is scarred,
by evil conscious
mathematics,
some beef is
everlasting,
some bonds can't be repaired,
some hearts can't be forgotten,

when the Lord's righteous are spent in the balance,
we must adapt a higher sense on behalf of poor righteous men
who stand close to the end time horizon's mist,
men claim to worship the
lord,
secretly live by their lustfulness and die by the sword,
these crooked men in white collars herald false prophet's
approach,
not justified, block manifestations of God's
righteous
reproach,
screw-faced
theologians
disrobing us
of spiritual armor,
holy men
send
soldier men with
paper thin
faith into battle,
searching after dollar signs,
lines of honor,
collars aligned,
it's designed
to harden scars,
in times
when people are

fearing transcendent
signs,
revelation of the ire
the whole episode
is on repeat

but I had to break
the fourth wall

before the captivity of misplaced hope
abused the sacred energy
given to me
by the formless
I Am

2007: When First I Entered The Vast And Arid Wilderness

XX. The Naked God (Saro'howet Oma'leu peh)

Somewhere between sunrise and sunset,
a veil exists,
we live each day in this nexus,
separated,

Sentience is illusion,
as is awareness, and life,

we are,
merely because we choose not to be absent,
even the saddest man around knows this,

I once knew what to say,
because I was at a place,
where I had heard all the words before,
it was whispered that we should take life as it
comes,

and so I took it and channeled it,
each afternoon in hidden alcoves,
living off lustful appendages of food,
and the regurgitation of what had been,

the design of a false perception,

Now we are at places, where we do not know
what to say,
our prophets have fallen,
revealed as mere sentience,
like we,

and therefore an illusion,

we await the Trumpet,
but the Mind never speaks,
though we speak to it,
we are much too foolish for all this mystery,
and much too brainwashed for the veil,

on a long enough time line,
eventually we all must go,

we live life fast,
in a world that hardly moves,
as mismatched
as socks and stockings,

There is a carrier universe between the soul divine
and the meta-person,
it is this with breeds the autonomy of life, the a,
and the b of logic.
This carrier universe is the intimacy and soul
which exists in the divine link between
humankind and their interpretation of God

we the foolish,
we the unknowing,
we exist in this carrier plane,
singing
"Take me where your loves goes,
don't run so far away,
whether rebel or saviour,
I'll always love You"

but the Veiled God recedes into places,
far too esoteric for our consumption,
far too upward for our equilibrium,

we are answered
in mysterious noises,
and dancing lights,

more pain than one being should feel,
this can't be all there is,

take off your Profoundness
show me You, without mystery,
an old book used by preachers and false prophets,
speaks of a man and a woman,
in a Garden,
and how they to God were naked, and thus wholly revealed,
would you return that favor,

and thus you be naked,
won't you in such profound nakedness
reveal yourself to me
and tell me where I am going
and what I am doing
those are the only two things of which
I am uncertain

XXI. I Am A Coward (Huj'om Wer'yup Kal'peh)

I realize
I have become a coward,
Running away from the demands of rebellion,
I don't feel pain, in moving on, I continue walking
And I keep living, at the cost of happiness and satisfaction

I count my friends on my hand, as I take the train,
In the morning to whatever expression that day will be

Do I still believe in the love of others?
They hurt me so deeply

My love is frail,
I am exile, vagabond,
king of ripped hearts

I am surrounded by a mist of green amber and turquoise,
we are lost in the riches and ambitions of a god,
But the heart of us is still black,
And the nature is still carnal,
Civilization is a delusion,
they are still barbarians in suit ties and hair gel,
mascara and high heels

Meat markets and spice trucks dot the rolling
plains and crackling deserts,
The waters, black oil,
smoke stacks and industrial revolutions,
Each person around me is the source of death
when he chooses to be a patriot to the corruptions,
I am not here to celebrate the rape of the world

no honesty in the life of love,
relationships based on complacence,
dysfunctional society and inebriated peoples,
delusional lives and empty connections

I am accountable for my own disillusion
because I have become a coward
Running away from the demands of rebellion
I don't feel pain,
In moving on, I continue walking, and
I keep living,
I just don't have the heart for pain
and I just don't want to cry
All I ever wanted was to be was a rebel with a
cause, yet
one soldier against the armies of human delusion
cannot win

XXII. The Refusal of the Embryo (Fu'manh Het)

Life As We Know It...

Diamonds are almost always found in spoiled milk,
if you know where to look,
and if you place your hand there, just right
a shock will kiss your bone as if your skin was air,

I stir man, liquefied in the orgasm of space,
psychedelic rips in the sky reveal a curious eye,
my tears flow out, rivulets of creation
like a crayon womb
I begat color,

a fly, the fire,
a shuttle into the sun,
we marinade into each other's destruction
to find birth,
even ecstasy isn't this good,

we play in serenades of the living,
crucified men who bathe and move in the grain of
death find elevation,
by dancing musical chairs to the marimba of our
consciousness,
exalted, nothing means nothing,
and here, nothing means anything,
we flow, a vibrant drumbeat,

we dry like freshly painted walls,

let go,
or eventually you will lose your mind,

we pursue infinity,
only because we die in a universe's moment,

we aborted the embryo,
with the beginnings of the see-through
indifference of dead men,

I look in the sky,
and see in the cosmos the beat of a tell-tale heart
that would make Edgar Allen Poe shiver and
reconsider his words

XXIII. Captor (Be'rahum pelao'tuom'h)

I have come to you tugging for air,
like a child born from a distant embryo,
to tell you that you have been deceived,

In a place that has already passed,
your deception was paid for and plotted by hands
which bore no marks,
and heads which bore no names

you have been placed in a cocoon,
in a land you do not know,
and told stories crafted by men which did not care,
since the dawn of the earth,

"This is life" you say, and blindly smile like a
mannequin in Milan,
or bons vivants in the high places,
chasing after doors and pathways,
which promise endless summers, and jets,
but you are the guilty one

truth is neither denied to you, nor concealed from
you,
you are a willing fool, a complacent whore among
energy,
it nags to you from behind the closed spaces of
your mind,

but you have blinded yourself to it

you pray to minstrels, and monks,
yet we and IT are each composed of energy,
you are blinded by green tea,
and loud choirs,
you are the guilty one, for truth is not denied you,

you let remain governments and lands which care
not for your progeny,
we speak in huddled corners about tragedies and
lies,
with a vendetta against a system which seeks to
feast on each of us,
but we complacently allow it,
you are the guilty one, for the truth is not denied
you,

we do not love each other,
somewhere in between codependency and
imitation, we are caught,
what is comfortable for you is comfortable for me,
contentment, fulfillment, joy, cast aside
you are the guilty one, for the truth is not denied
you,

and in the end, when humankind collapses the
universe with its mind,
and all things come to pass,

who shall remain but the energy,
geishas of power, dancing and speaking in tongues,
which will speak of us in cordial tongues and regretful chords, saying,
"There once stood man, our greatest tragedy, and our greatest hope".

see with your inside eye,
or it will all be over,

take this knowledge,
and plant this seed:
we were never born,
and in essence we shall never die,
because we never lived

Life is not life without truth

XXIV. For Certain (Wum'jahu oi'lum a'pi)

There's nothing I know,
For certain

But I question the notion that there is a devil,
He who yins the yang of evil, and stares coldly at love,
I don't believe, and to the creed of his existence I refuse,
You are the one who twists history,
I am the one who butchers life,
You are the one who rapes serenity,
I am the one who pillages anatomy autonomously for love,
You are the one who knifes mercy,
I am the one who kills men,
We are the ones who defile our self,
We are the ones who are guilty,
There is no singular force,
But it is the conscience of humankind,
The spirit of us
You are Adam, yes, you are Adam,
you are Serpent, you are Shiva, and you are Anubis
We are accursed,
And I wonder if God still exists in the realm

Who/What
Real/Where
You are the lust,
I am the prejudice,

We are the pain of the world,
We are accursed, I believe

There's nothing I know,
For certain

They are men for whom the whole world is
papyrus,
And, with blood-ink and bone-pen, they write,
Like a hurricane upon sandy bark they twist the
natural into leprosy,
Like fire upon the skin of men, they deteriorate
creation into scar,
Like disease in the healthy, they are the ones who
ravage the constructed,
the creation-infants with small minds who scale
the stars,
we, the barbarians who presume civility,
we, the beginners who call ourselves
grandmasters, we...
It seems, dogs are the only ones capable of love
unfettered,
but even they are flawed,
Perversion like those who sit and write of
revolution
but do nothing about it,
Perversion like those who study scripture and writ
but never change,
I am so tired of revolts and spirituality
among a world for whom none of it is real,
Bring Soweto to my street corner

or bring destruction to this whole earth,
Bring revelation,
or ravage this earth with that power which is
beyond the nuclear,
This was never real, you see,
this was never real..

We live and believe,
But only exist for what we live and believe in at
peaks of time,
And then we coalesce,

If you believe, go, you, look into this fire and cast
yourself into it,
gasolined,
and burn, like as to the fire of conviction, made
mortal in doom,
If you believe,
allow yourself to churn with the sea water and do
not fight it,
like as to the churning of struggle, made sentient
in mortality,
This was never real, you see,
It was never real

Do you see where your limits are drawn, in the
moderation,
void of extreme,
This is not real, do you see...

Faith is like unto the clouds,

it is used by those who do not really believe
to give them a thing to hold on to,
yet,
Belief, blind and stupid and foolish,
it is all I want

Make this life better, Nameless
I cannot take mystery, Spirit?
It? One? What should I call you?
Are you even there?

I do not find you in a book anymore,
I do not see you in a religion now,
I have discovered that they are all lies,
I cannot take this hypocrisy
all flawed, all skewed,
you are not dragon,
you have not many arms,
you are not wind,
you are not man's comprehension,
so what do I call you, where do I find you,
are you ever there,
do you ever care?

Humankind? We? Us? What should I call you?
Are we ever real?
I do not find you in the flesh beings who surround
me
with their presence-energy,
You are not mother,
You are not father,

nor brother,
You are not sister,
You are not teacher,
You are not preacher,
You are not leader,
nor lover,
So what do I call you, where do I find you,
are you ever there?
what are we?

Unanswered questions will undo me,
And unanswered prayers will seal the deal

There's nothing I know,
For certain

And that leaves me cold right through...
-the sun extinguishes,
the earth's core shudders,
the stars die,
and fire becomes an unattainable god again-

Cold right through...

I, the intellectual,
I, the philosopher,
I, the man,
I, the lover,
I, the teacher,
I, the friend
I, the me,

Me
I
?

I fear,
I, the phony,
I, the liar,
I, the double life,
I, the false prophet,
I, the double-tounged,
I, the double edged sword,
I, the insane,
I, the preposterous,
I, the actor,
I, the symbiotic

The only thing that stays this knife at my throat,
The shard at my wrist,
This gas at my foot,
This noose at my neck,

Is
I, the hoper,
I, the giver,
I who, for once in my fucking life, want to know something real,
want to know something void of mystery and faith and illogical,
and weird ritual,
I want to know people as past human:
beings, who in being are thus more than those

who only live for life's sake

I who want to know the world as paradise,
to know life as life,
There has to be more than this,

And the only thing that stays me from giving into
the insanity
that would feel ever so good,
The demise that might comfort me,
The destruction...
Is
The I, whom even the leeches call "good spirit"
Perhaps there is a purpose to all this

If I'm so good, though, then help me,
Why not help me?

I say I won't do it again, a lie,
I say I won't stray again, a lie,
But I also ask for strength, where is it?
I ask for You, where are You?
I know "free will" but what about intervention for
the foolish
I don't know how much more I can take,
how much longer I can do this

There's nothing I know,
For certain
Me

There's nothing I know,
For certain
You

There's nothing I know,
For certain
Earth

There's nothing I know,
For certain
God

There's nothing I know,
For certain
Life

There's nothing I know,
For certain

There's nothing I know,
For certain

XXV. Rebel or Saviour (Seiʼsa leʼanutph aiʼtuh)

I despise finding the words,
My life has begun whispering prayers to an old
Catholic rosary
Isn't that enough?

These days, I defy catharsis,
I only want resurrection

I heard the prayers from the hanged man at sunset
on the eve of judgment
I heed the words

I am become Ethereal
I am become Apocalypse
A child points to redemption, beating like a drum
In those who walk in it and teach from it
Outreaching and moaning in the soul

One shard of noir, colors like the nostalgia of burnt
apple slices,
Light from the sunset as it streams through
raindrops,
Individual crystals shattering the light into colors,
Each drop of rain becomes a million rainbows,
Falling from the sky

Looking into one, I see myself, as I was and as I am

I wonder which version of me was the best

They who introduced me to sin sit high in a cell of their construction
Rightfully so

The moon crashes into the earth as a mad dragon feasts upon the stars,
Like a god drunk off the spirits and the drugs of an infinite being,
I see millions of individual paths before me

Drugged frenzy, trance, dreamworld, a state of being
Perfect and imperfect connection with the entire universe,
each path is the sand grain on the beach of my collective futures,
I see millions of paths that end in my redemption, my fame, my ministry, my happiness, my sadness, my suicide, my life, my change,
I even see the paths which to lead to my death,
Weep your tears, because unfortunately, unbeknownst to me is which of those paths I am walking

this is the language of the utmosts,
which lie deep in the granular space of a being

Eat your bread, and learn from
The Path Maker, The World Weaver,
The Transverses, the Conduit,
The Receptacle, The Plane Crosser,
The Intimate

Awareness
In flashes, I have become aware of how the world
treats its prophets
Like beings, souls must be gestated,
like an unborn child,
or, like that unborn child un-nurtured,
the soul itself is miscarried into nothingness,

Truth: I am resentful of them for what they did to me.
Truth: I had grown to hate relationships with most people in the world
Truth: You caused me so much pain, yet I have found so much redemption.
Truth: Maybe I am uncanny figure. Maybe I am a prophet. Maybe I am a revolutionary. Perhaps a delusional madman with delusions of grandeur I do not possess

But you should love me, no matter what
Why do you search so hard for love, when you can seek your love nearby,
Don't you see I build my life around you,

I wonder if this is the unhealable wound of which they speak,
I love you, whether you are my rebel or my savior,
whether you kill and mock, or destroy to rebuild,
and whatever you choose to be, it really doesn't matter to me,
because I'm going to love you,
spreading rose petals over the water and
writing haiku to old mystics, ancient drunks, prophets, whores, and monks, walking to all that awaits

2008: When First I Became Lost In The Mirages

XXVI. Kinetic Slavery: Love As Religion (Se'luwoh A'um Vl'eop)

I.

I do not presume to guess the consciousness
which leads me,
But like liquid sin in a jealous pond,
I am inebriated, I have no freedom,
carelessly I interpret every sacrifice made
as a beacon to call me closer
you have become the spot on the sun,
after one stares too long
I envision you in ideas that swell and
burst in orgasmic colors, wordless,
you are flowers carefully strewn across the eyes of
blind merchants,
it's not what you see or know,
but what you hear that makes you dangerous,
you arrest civilization in a capsule of your design,
like narcotics,
a dread angel abandoned in minute escapes,
I am blown away and therefore lost in orange
slices and amber,
I have become the ambrosia and nectar
which you sip from a cup and grab from a bronzed
bowl,
you stir me in a pot on a table, and laugh carelessly
soaking in the light of something called
(unmentionable),

far more cosmic and potent then the sun, I am your slave,
so much so that my passions last night were ignited and
betrayed by your silhouette

II.
Sweltering pieces of your heart shatter my defenses,
like the cracked tongue of one lost in a desert dream world, thirsty,
bathed in sand and blue,
you are the master of my future and the realization of my past,
sophisticated copper glasses align the entrance to the temple,
and by drinking from these cups,
I break the seal of captivity and create temporary manmade freedoms for myself,
imprisoning my captivator, giving me the chance to escape,
a chance I never take and can't embrace
I betray you in a river of painful anomalies,
shouted in curse words across a street in Manhattan,
Your voice smells of lavender and turmeric,
preparing me for a Grecian orgy with entire civilizations of beauty,
I compare your tears to golden light,

and these tears break my heart in countless ways,
countless times,
each broken lie you weave around me, I believe,
even to the last one
I promised that I would rip the world apart
to its foundations before you enthralled me again,
but you conceive ever impressive wishful thoughts
for me,
comparing my expression to nothingness,
and building a throne made of stimulation
to deny the corruption of your touch,
with such speed one might never land if one
jumped,
you catch me, and I awake in a wound of the most
sincere
and piteous delight,
a wound in the fabric of the consciousness that
held me,
you won't allow me victory
pointing a finger at me, you marry me to
inebriation,
pressed close to me you offer sunflowers, sparks,
signs, dreams, and love,
even as you pick over the remains of hope,
I should like to think that I would call for help
but what sense would it make to cry out in a place
where even the air is your command,
My eyes open once in a while to reveal
that we are in a subway in Harlem now,

you have no boundaries and bedeck me
with lawlessness and fornication,
It is a heresy even for me to question the heresies we commit,
if I could but be freed once more to chase the Light
I would offer a flower to my hero,
perhaps in time, I will gain resolve,
and your chains will weaken, but this is not that day,
You claim to love but leave me with battle scars,
You love the look of my wounds

III.

In a Dream
I cast wishes on the floor before me like colored touches,
and moving caresses, imploring that you return to me the sunlight,
for here stuck in starshine's rays, I know pain,
Sands blow across my weary face,
etching stone hardened tales of a lost embrace,
Stuck in a moment, forgotten instantly,
here stands an apocalyptic breaking of two hearts
interlinked by self-inflicted suffering,
show me a way to get the sunshine back,
lost in the point between two oceans,

IV.
a mist overcame me,

and in a vision I saw the paradise, divine inspired,
a land of perpetual sun,
where the light stays always for fear that
nighttime's eye blind you
to the treasure to be found there,
the stars and the aurora
playing games of chase and pursuit in the sky,
honey flowed down the streets in a stream
side by side with pure water,
and at times they interlinked without ever
touching,
a field of sugarcane,
a pasture of cherry trees
plums, mangoes, and all tropical creations,
all animals, vicious and true, stood side by side
leading me toward a temple
which was the only building in the land,

following to where they lead I enter the temple,
and entering, behold only an altar,
where my soul lies with a dagger above it,
Looking out of the glassless window, I see you
eyeing the dagger and me,
you hold up gold and coral,
and diamonds to keep my eyes from the dagger
slowly falling,
The air before me shimmers, and it is you there
now
You take my hand,

And in my mind
I see images of days to come, days that are,
days that were, days that might have been,
I see desolations,
I see the first wasteland, the last paradise,
I see all things beautiful near all things corrupt,
At your mercy, let me be,
As I cannot hold these things within

V.
I see hate and blind loyalty,
pride and conceit,
the green eyes of a leopard of hate,
a wolf chewing on the carcass of a hyena,
I see things of great evil which cannot be described
with earthly words,
that writhe, and moan, and seep, and die

VI.
I see death and life stand side by side
begging me choose
if I do not release myself from this,
You will destroy me, a final marking point,
Destruction vis-à-vis the desperate need for
validation,
Masquerading as love,
You are the beautiful death,
The careful suicide,

So many years of my life have been dedicated to you
I always knew it was a simple as a choice,
But it's the easy choices that cause the most pain,
The simple struggles that are the hardest to defeat

VII.
Finally,
Though the empty sadist in me would have stayed forever,
I choose life
And choice's causality forces you to release my hand,
You walk out of the temple leaving me there,
a willing sinner finally begging for redemption,
my soul, still on the altar, is unscathed by the dagger,
which left with you,
It rises from the altar and walks into me,
The essence of my soul connecting with the atoms of my person once more,
Your love is slavery
Right down to the core
You are the beautiful death, the careful suicide,
But I chose life

a veil at the back of the temple,
transports me through a luxurious emptiness,
a void composed of

resplendent rivulets of all colors,
that, dissipating,
returned me to the place I originated,
and the lack of captivity is like a fear filled silence
which I never knew

I have much to relearn, because it's been captivity
Right down to the core

XXVII. Suihallawuiyou (or The Girl At Ota'lu'kume) (A Vision) (Art Piece Representing Mental Breakdown and Recovery)

This is the ninth time the altar has been broken

And the sky itself is broken across my hands,
I'd been out chasing the girl at the river for so long,
I did not realize she was a ghost of what she had been
incense from the temple dances in,
rising in curls of transcendent intangibility,
a color like grey, but blue,
a blue sky, and a singular sunflower,
bending from the frost,
a weed grows nearby as the soil plots the sunflower's funeral,
rainbows across her eyes, blindfolded by years,
I did not know she was but a whisper of what she once had been,
the gong sounds, as I purify the water by the bay,
and the waterfalls nearby attract dancing butterflies,
that follow the course of the river into the bay,
where the ship slides sensually across the water,
leaving ripples behind that will go on to tell the faraway waters about the people on the ship, their lives, their souls, their dreams, their sins

I have seven pieces of gold

Whisper

Time Changes

Dancing Light

I WATCH THE WANDERER

I. The Betrothal of the Nomad Wanderer (A Legend)

He who walks across the sun-burned desert,
his journey began in lush prairies, before his eyes were covered with dust,
there before him is a palace of rubble, a fallen city,
the priest points to the tower and speaks words,
but the Wanderer cannot hear,
he writes on papyrus with charcoal a simple message

The First Haiku- Implore
I would know the land
Impart your knowledge to me
I will fly away

and the priest spoke, dipping a bamboo stick in water,
as the ripples disturbed the moonflowers,
a reverberating chime echoes across the water

The Second Haiku- Sympathy
You who wish to fly
The mountains are far from here
Go through the rubble

The rubble fell away,
the Wanderers hands moving in between the time
of the existence of the rubble,
the sky is broken across my hands,
but I follow him shaking beads and throwing rice,
The Mothers celebrate the children, who go to war,
but the sky is fallen, and the moon remains,
the sun is taunting the fourth house, in the realm of day

II. Vagabond
He who was the Wanderer
is bought with new oil,
new love, new presence,
the Enemy sends the Vagabond to tempt him
Rose petals fly through the air, as the cyclone rips apart the
village, the candle is consumed in its own fire,

as the wax falls atop the incense smoke,
the Lovebirds mate atop the mountain which spews lava,
before they too are consumed,
civilizations make tales of their noble love and tragic demise,
the priest picks a moonflower, and sends it
the double creation, the triple conclusion,
the singular want for love

The Third Haiku- Temptation
Blood spilled on one want
the temple of thieving hearts
I wait there for you

Flesh of a man, there is no simple way to please you,
love rising like the veil parted on Jezebel,
Babylon fell only to rise again,
the Vagabond must be sent away,
for he has become a hyena, calling name and laughing,
the Wanderer must see through deception

The Fourth Haiku- Wisdom
Essence of rose seed
there is no temple but truth
Yours is gone astray

The Vagabond was sent away

The girl dancing by the Bay

I did not know she was but a shell of what she
once had been,
and the fire is near burnt out
She ties a white cloth around her fourth finger on
her left hand,
I do the same

Ceremony of betrothal

Colors on white snow, light is the air that
surrounds the aurora,
nebula shining brilliant,
swimming in the water,
you might not weep so much, if you seek the sun
This is the ninth time the altar has been broken

III. The Seventh War
Flags of every nation, broken is the heart of man
love of peace surrendered breeds life for they who
hate the world
the center of the skies sings of flowers bent in oil,
it is this which the girl wants

I have seven pieces of gold
Who do you care for these days,

what do you truly love

The Fifth Haiku- Wonder
Betroth sky and earth
you undertake the most
the reward is great

Burning the flesh of the wolf, the Wanderer eats,
yet a pulsing light, at the center of the peaks
near the mountain calls him, to the place of
surrender,
of the pack of men, he never was a member
I will bedeck you with promises of the magic
realm
where the girl at Ota'lu'kume has received the
scroll
Ota'lu'kume is the place where logic meets chaos
and from it chaos is dispelled
Chaos dispelled itself, for peace's sake
like water bends to whatever object it is placed in,
so you must,
to find the bread of intelligence gathered, the
peace of secret love,
and the desire of the wondered joy

Mi'ts'sukiami
is the word that best described the secret world
logic without logic, this is a secret language
dreams are spread before the ground, upon desire

do you walk,
the secret world this is all you could ever want

The Sixth Haiku- Secret Manifold
The world of frost fire
you do not know the true way
manifold it is

A pot of grain, you cut the jugular, I will cut the legs,
tonight we have meat for dinner, the other cows left to graze
Whisper blue like ocean tides and bid farewell to the dream of the Enemy,
he is no more,
do you still swear allegiance to this

I will bedeck you with the secret world
Behold the secret language which transcends time and place

The First War-Haku'tiawa (A Circle With A Bolt of Lightning)
Man behold the first war, sword against sword
the tree is cut down, smoke rises,
gasoline rainbows in puddles across Harlem

The Second War- Mish-um'uitl (A Triangle, With A Circular Rectangle, And A Dot)

The girl at Ota'lu'kume saw the second war, blood spilled,
mystery beheld, from the Eastern rise to the Falling Day,
Green Bay, Whispered thieves
THOSE WHO LOVED US BETRAYED US
The thieves run from truth

The Third War- Katwil'awai'wawei'waeeeii (A Slashing line, in a
triangle)
Judas, Pilate, and Brutus at the last levels of hell,
do not betray,
oh humankind, do not betray

The Fourth War- Nis'it'wilaweeii (A Thick Circle,
with a sunflower
dipped in water)
the truth of peace is where you least expect it

The Fifth War- Mis'ss'um'partumus (A candle burning with butterflies dancing around it, a singular woman wearing a robe, singing the siren song of Ota'lu'kume)
Love for Love given, Kiss for Kiss given, peace for peace given, Don't you see

TRUMPETS

There should be no need for war

The Sixth War- Nis'cutar (Nectar over a people
with redemption)
Freedom, conformed, kind words,
sweet tidings to all who know the truth

The Seventh War- Sui'hamma'ui'ti'la'wiyouma(All
Things Captive, Are Set Free)
The Wanderer finds the pulsing mountain at the
peaks

IV. Finale
Time Changes

Love

First Person

Peace

I BECOME THE WANDERER'S EYES

The girl stands at the pulsing light, I did not know
she was a
fragment of what she once had been
She wrote me a letter on charcoal

The Seventh Haiku
I am completed
My journey and your pure quest
We are one again

She spoke one thing more

For our home and the linking of our spirits I need seven pieces of gold to pay the gatekeepers, the pathmakers, and the watchers who know the CREATOR

I spoke

It is all that I have, and all that I have is yours

We are reunited, made one again,
We dance, and we dance
My true love

2009: When First I Found Water In The Desert

XXVIII. The Logistic of If/Then (Keta'sep 1)

If love, then harmony
If peace, then war,
if war, then death,
if order, then chaos,
Rationality is a derivative of perception,
perception a part of logic, logic apart of awareness,
wilt thou be captured unawares

if vanity, then pride
if pride, then demise,
what is thy desire?

if worldly desire, worldly consequence,
if transcendent necessity, then transcendent reward,
existence is perception, physics is spirituality,
metaphysics is universal soul searching,
toward heavenly plains we march

if consequence, then wisdom,
if wisdom, then refrain
if refrain, then moderation,
if moderation, then peace,
renunciation is a reigning indicator of peace,
peace is only from surrender

if rambling, then foolish,

if foolish, then demise,
in demise, return is cruel and arduous a road to walk,
in return, before thy demise, turn, and, to peace, return

a virtuosic whisper dedicated to one ear, this is your path, follow it
a blood-stained sword dedicated to one army, this is you future, follow it,
a burned flag raised above abandoned lands, this is your sign, follow it
only chosen people shall know of revolution, this is your providence, follow it

If consequence, then reason,
if reason, then thought,
if thought, then action,
if action, then preparation,
prepare thyself humble, and anoint thyself well,
beyond this gate you kicked down, many more remain to fall

If blocked then broken,
if broken, then removed,
if removed, then walked,
if walked, then known,
one may talk about things and things to come,
but one can only walk to the result

if seen, then heard,
heard, then known,
if both, then known,
if thrice, then felt
if thou shalt see and hear, and feel,
and know of revolutions and war cries to come,
choose the side for which thy shall fight,
for on battle lines, none can choose anew

if incense is potion, then potion is word
if word is desire, then desire is ocean
if ocean is sea, then sea is river,
river bending towards the brook upon which my shack sits,
and in my shack shalt thy find herbs and tonic and brew and food
upon which thou can eat, if thy only have a word with me,
of things that were, of things that are, of things that are to come,
of things that are all three simultaneously,
you have free will, then choose to know of such things

if laugh, then cry
if cry, then tears,
if tears, then smile,
if smile, then the soul is free,

cast aside all chains, this is the only place you
could want,
already the world melts away

if logic, then rationale,
if rationale, then awareness,
if awareness, then question,
if question, then thou shalt surely die,
how can thy ask question of things which thou
dost not know,
and cannot know, and will not know,
and know not of things which thou should know

here lies the rationality of existence:
irrational is code,
illogical is desire,
perception is existence,
existence is perception,
both are freely given,
let all be freely used,
and when the time shall come,
all shall be freely known,
and all shall be free told,
and all shall be freely known,
and all shall be free, and freely known
and all shall be
and all shall
and all
and

Illogical ending to logical statement,
rationality has no place here,
metaphysical design upon universal truth,
knowledge is only good if one shall use it
and one shall only use it if for the truth
the truth,
in truth

XXIX. I See Without Time (Si'lahu so'phet qua'heht)

I. Psalm

The song of eternity is balanced upon my fingertips,
It is the light of the dawning sun captured in the dew upon my nail,
I see paradise in your vulnerabilities,
a world in your tearful surrender,
A gentle rain and the cargo of Jerusalem is captured in spice and seed,
I behold torrential sandstorms in a place of no location,
I see without time
The rebirth

Mercy be upon the woeful
and blessed is the heart of the corrupt who know Redemption
Guardian, Your words are each a new birth of the metaphysical
Guardian, You are several higher souls
Guard the sun and moon from the film of murky black
Fuel the heart of humankind to dream without logic
To know without distrust
For the souls stolen,

spellbound in a web of troubles
Spread ashes from the Tropics unto the snow,
these opposites,
and in the opposites, let moderation
garner equality in the places where the soul is
captured in unbalance

Bring righteousness
There are tears
I have discovered

Completions come like the clouds in the sky,
and they go,
leaving behind the stark contrast of western sun
against raining gloom,
the red light spilt upon the trees crackling
kinetically
in the mind,
against the melancholic grey clouds holding their
purifying water,
Green emeralds and the peace of a rose dash back
and forth
between your lusts,
and righteous desires

Bring renewal
If even at the price of the universe
These are tears for the luminous

These are moans for dark

I see without veils
and without law

I see without time
Twilight awaits,
therefore choose well
Chase the sun

Guardian,
Even now
I see without time

II. A Prayer
Mercy be upon the woeful,
who do not dream but for fear of its deferring
and within the time upon which is marked the
years of nostalgia's fancy,
let such peace, the peace of that age,
the age of number and age of time,
gain the equilibrium to travel forward to the day of
life,
and the life-marked days woven in the golden
future

III. The Preacher
I met it and have seen it:
the twilight which wisdom warns of

I know and have experienced the sliding back into
regretful
circumstances,
as if in wish of the disastrous pleasure found there

It is from this point on that we must know grace,
and in such grace,
mercurially pursue the sunsets of happiness to
come,
Who has forgotten the battle which wages in the
tongue of man,
and in the nature of man's heart,
the origin of man's nature is cuffed away from
beautification,
by the desire for freedom,
freedom by separation
disconnected from the Function of Creativity,
the Connection with the Origin Being

Power is in the authority that humankind gives,
sharing, from person to person

Lost are those wrapped in the slavery of dominion

2010: When First I Returned From My Pilgrimage

XXX. The Places I Know Of (Suma hotatu pawi umaro'met)

Believe me...
I know of places,
accessible only to the dream,

The occasional dream
Set'maalu Te'hutapl Ot

I believe some deity has mercy on me,
Some ancient god left behind, unmoved by science
and cynicism,
Or perhaps some medicine healer or witchdoctor
who lives two blocks down,
Some force can feel when I am broken,
And at night opens this place to me

I know of places, believe me, accessible only to the
dream

A city
Strong like an old kingdom
Built like a favela
Houses like rooms in the compound
No roofs
People live there, I'm sure
Clothing blows in the breeze,
The smell of food,
Chicken, herbs, and green vegetation,
Spiced,
A thin beach at the edge of the favela,

Sweet tan sands

The sky and water the same sapphire,

The sky-waters move gently,
But never overcome the city,
Making love with the sand,

If there are storms,
I am never there when they come,

I know of places,
believe me,
accessible only to the dream,

White cumulus cloud-mountains,
Full and bulbous,
Floating through, and adoring the water-sky

It was in emptiness that I discovered
the roadway, a laser beam aimed
diagonally up passing the stratosphere

Like the source magic of my ancestors,
Mixing herbs and paste for healing

I found repair, walking that roadway
Until I had stepped off the Earth,

And leaving the atmosphere, I was caressed
By that ...-ness

A living being, it embraced me,
And at once beyond this planet,
I was on all worlds

Energy lasciviously vibrated my atoms
And held me suspended
A world made of light
There is an occasional dream

XXXI. The Transfiguration of Breath (Sa'atahlp Etahuamet Ka'Sephml O')

When I have been broken, I have sighed...

Heated by the warmth of the flesh from which
they were expelled,
Those sighs rise in the air,
Until they color the sky a hue like hopeless,

In the wind,
My exhalations of lament circle the globe,
Entwining with twisters on the plains,
Hurricanes on the coasts,

In the breeze they travel,

And occasionally in the redness of sun,
I stand outside, face upward,
and the breeze upon which they ride strikes my
cheek,
Drenching me in melancholy,
A malaise unshakeable,
Momentary,
But memorable
I mark those moments, for those sighs have
returned to me

If there is an ancient, forgotten god,
circling the earth in a chariot, bearing a cosmic
calendar as his avatar,

Those sighs have risen to him by now,
and my mournful exhalations have marked those
broken days-past upon that calendar,
And engrained their representation of the suffering
I have experienced into the flesh of the time-
universe,
Representing all that I have lost,
The disappearance of all that I had hoped for,

Once my sighs have reached the end of the of the
atmosphere and the edge of the world, they must
circle back down in the cycle of the air-spheres,
Traveling the globe once more,
Whispering to all who will listen about the pain
that I have endured,

I posit that the breeze contains the
Gentle melancholic gasps of myself, and the
millions like me,
Who perch upon the dock, stand upon the shore,
wait upon the pier,
Hoping to see the sails of our ship,
which has not yet come

And again, occasionally,
As I move through the world,
A breeze will strike my cheek,
And I can feel it,
And I know it,
And I recognize that it contains the breath from
the sighs I exhaled, when I was broken,

Because energy has a signature,
And energy never dies,
And like-energies stay close,

As all energy has a signature,
And energy never dies,
And like-energy stays close
I know my sighs in the wind,
I recognize them each time they pass me,

I used to let them travel the world, carrying the remembrance of my suffering to faraway lands that I might never see,
Touching distant people I might never meet,
Skimming remote waters I might never sail,

And now I've tired of reliving the suffering each time my sighs past me in the wind,
I've tired of being marked by all the ways I was hurt and all the ways I hurt,
I've tired of leaving my pain in the wind to touch others with the same anguish and misfortune

I'll not let them stay there any longer...

And so I went to Bullfrog Lake,
And I climbed the high hill which they use for sledding during the winter season when the snow falls,

And I sat there, and waited until I sensed my sighs
in the wind,

For days I sat there,
And the park ranger would come to me,
Recognizing me from my previous journeys
through these woods and up this hill,
And he would sit with me,
And ask me if I was well,
And I would tell him,
"Here is a work that I must do!"
And he would leave me,
For he could see in my eyes that I would not leave
until this work had been done

And finally, after some time,
as the breeze blew past, I could see my old sighs
coming with them,
Because they are a hue like hopeless,
And I know the color well,
for it has long been my banner,
And as my sighs sought to rush past me, I looked
at them,
And with all the power of the universe, the infinite
realization of What I Am, and What We Are, And
What Is,
I willed the wind around my sighs into a pocket of
air, trapping them there,
The way the meteorologists describe the weather,

And stuck in that near intangible chamber, held by
my will,
The wind could carry them no further,

And I willed that chamber to me,
And though no other eyes could detect it,
I could see the wind chamber carrying the sighs
I've exhaled for years coming toward me,
And when it was in front of me,
within arm's reach,
I put my left hand into that pocket of air, piercing
it like an abscess, that I might extract and purify
the old and familiar and invisible toxicity inside,
And with my hand inside that pocket,
I wove my sighs around it until I wore them like a
glove,

Then I withdrew my hand,
And like reiki healing,
I moved my right hand around my sigh-gloved left
hand in gentle circles,
And I chanted, and incanted, and willed, and
invoked, and runed, and charmed, and conjured,
And I sang hymns, and meditated,
And from my right hand I Changed the melancholy
of my past sighs, extracting the pensive gloom,
Atom by atom,
Until my left hand was gloved by nothing more
than air,

And gently, I uncircled that air from my left hand
and released it back into the wind,
Like a ribbon of oxygen

And from that,
I have learned to gather my sighs as soon as they
leave my mouth,
And purify them if they are sad,
that I contribute nothing to the world except that
which will feed and uplift it,

And even more,
I have learned to sigh less,

And I have learned to avoid the things,
Which will make me sigh in suffering,

And now, I chase after things,
Which will make me sigh in joy and awe,

And those sighs of joy and awe…those sighs…

I let blow in the wind for as long as they like

2012: Songs For A Defining Year Of My People &
My Generation

XXXII. The Breakdown of Matter (Komo Ummaet L'kuawol)

...and how dare you demand that rot be beautiful

Dogma creates programming and conditioning which demands
That Black pain must be palatable, peaceful,
That the blood of our children be vibrant paint for your canvas,
That the skin of infants be formed into native wraps,
That the scent of our dead be sweet perfume,
That the tears of our living be a warm laughing river for you to swim in,
That our flesh be a costume for you to pantomime,
That our bones be luxurious fossil,
That our horror and fear be inoffensive,
That our cries to whatever deity will listen be silent,
That we remain the hidden untouchables in an Unacknowledged caste

But when has decomposition been kind?

it is the ravaging of life now dead,
and you must suffer the stench

my tears will not moisturize your skin,
they are born of centuries of suffering

does it surprise you they are acidic and corrosive
when they fall like rain on the ground,

our wails will not be in tempo or melody,
atonal and free-rhythm:
we cry for those
for whom concrete was a final lover,
for whom asphalt was the last bed,
for whom a knee to the head & the weight of a
body on the cranium
were the caress which escorted
the soul into the next realm

bullet through flesh produces a song which you
must bear,
the snapping of lynched necks writes a verse you
must recite
suffering will not adhere to your terms

that which you have killed will decompose
the skin must turn black, the muscle die away
the blood to a hard paste apothecary
the bones to earth
how dare you demand that agony be silent

no more than you can control the rising of smoke
from incense
can you control the screams of those still living in
a prison made
of the tissues, sinews, & corpuscles of those they
loved

We are peaceful shaman people,
Born from shaman, mystics, and astronomers,
And we hold in our core a vision,
bathed in golden light,
a vision more delicate than the scent of lilac on a windy day,
a vision of spirits connected on a higher plateau,
reflecting that unity here in this plane,
linked while we inhabit these human vessels,
from generation to generation,
until our progeny are like One Being,
interdependent, connected,
psychically harmonious

A vision we pray becomes reality

We pray for an era that never ends where
peace is the fiber, the framework, the fabric of our permanence,
Halcyon, bucolic

In the interim…
We will not embalm the aroma of our decomposing children,
You must inhale the fetor,

we will mark your spirit with the final violent memories of our lost,
so the Deities will deny you entrance into the sun,
and while here in this realm

you must endure the skin-rending minor key of
our cries
like agriculturists on the social plantation, cultural
terra-formers
we will march and move
until the disintegration ends

until then...
...how dare you demand that rot be beautiful

XXXIII. Womyn's Sad Hymn Against Birth (Set'ku Pajhmu Karom'l)

Womyn weeping, kneeled, her eyes translating
through the veiled liquidity of tears,
laying before her,
staining, with blood, the freshly paved tax-paid street,
her child, now dead,
yet once this human mound was living flesh
which had split from her I Am
into existence,
which she had loved into advancement,
from chrysalis to the capability of flight,
self-sufficiency and aspiration,

her child, now robbed of dotage

looking at her now-gone-child,
she thought of the many ways he could have died
before this moment,
and she prayed, in vain,
for the chariot of time to swing backward

she wished her child had died at any moment
before this one,

fate would have been kinder to take her child in youth,
than for her child to die here in the street,
in a murder that would be excused and accepted,

because the guns that ripped his soul & flesh from
his body
bore serial numbers marking them official
property of the city,
tools of those sworn-in-oath to preserve

she wished for infertility,
that the ultrasound had revealed nothing but the
normal churning of digestion instead of the
fermenting of life,
that her eggs had been unsound and incapable of
fertilization,
of splitting cell unto cell unto cell unto newness,
that her uterus was a place of acid and impossible
temperatures
like the atmosphere of Venus,
the planet named for the very goddess to whom
Womyn is compared

she wished that her fallopian tubes were blocked
by a tumor or cellular plaque,
that her womb was a Black Mass, a space of death
and emptiness,

she wished that the fetus that she had fed with her
own blood would have aborted itself within her,
malnourished, doomed

she wished that the baby she created would have
died at birth,
complications from breech, or still born,

she wished that the doctor would have
mishandled the baby,
breaking its neck or back, or dropping it, head
first, on the hard tile floor of the birthing room

she wished that the child would have died in its
crib,

She wished that the child had did in youth, at the
playground,
stricken by a car, lightning, or a terminal disease

a falling branch, a roving gang war,
an unforeseen explosion, a genetic complication
a building collapse, an earthquake,
a tornado, a falling satellite,

Womyn
on her knees in the street,
holding her now-grown, now-dead child,
in her hands,
many tiny rivers of blood running,
pouring from the sources of open wounds,
holes in the flesh left from flying pieces of metal,
skin-burningly hot from the speed of their
ejection,
bullets sprayed like the ejaculation of racism's lust
deep into the flesh of her child

she moaned, violent contractions in her stomach
from the uncontrollable sobbing,
contractions that reminded her of the ones she
experienced when she gave birth to the life which
lay expired and infinite now,
before her,
a horizontal crucifixion,
death as art:
Grown Child On Concrete, Steal Life
Dead flesh as sculpture, pavement as canvas

as cameras ate the flesh of the moment,
preparing to regurgitate it into the psyche of the
unbothered masses at home,
reporters gathering news,
yellow tape, an item of magic transfiguration,
transforming this intersection into a
scene to be investigated
by the very humans responsible for making
her child's body the central piece

As she screamed, hoping her soul
would leave her body with the forceful wails,
and join the now-gone spirit of her child

as she used her bare hands like washrags to wipe
her child's blood,
like the washrags she once used to wash the
child's living body years ago,

as she kneeled before her child,

tempted to run at the people who took him
in the hopes they would fire upon her
taking her as well

yes,
as she looked at her now-gone-child,
she thought of the many ways he could have died
before this moment

and she prayed, in vain,

she wished her child had died before birth:
for it would have been kinder,
than for her child to die here in the street,
in murder that will be excused and accepted,
because the guns that ripped his soul from his
body
bear serial numbers marking them official property
of the city,
tools of those sworn-in-oath to preserve

Womyn,
kneeling over the dead flesh that she bleed life
into,
sang a sad hymn
against child-birth

XXXIV. Nebula Being (Sora Tui Teh'impko Wa'a O)

Nebula Being,
You match the first hue of infinity

Black you are the start,
The color of the All before This as we know it,
before the great We Are that sparked life,
Before light, water, blood & soul,
and the moist vapor of breath ,
Blackness, you existed,
matching the beginning of time

Black you are the last,
You are the color of the collapse of this universe
into the next phase of existence,
When all the stars have died and all energy has
been extinguished,
When illumination terminates,
When the fabric of matter & time crumble into
kinetic transformation,
Blackness, when there is nothing, you will exist,
You match transfiguration

Even when the dominating entities, in hatred,
take away our matter:
Nebula Being,
You exist,
A substance for the birth of all things

Remember this

When you are alone,
In cold rooms,
On cold Earth,
In silence,
Disconnected,
On the brink of sanity,
On a starless night,
When there is no moon,
unilluminated,
When you encounter the tunnel where there is
no ending light,
When hours have passed
and morning has not come
Remember this,
In those moments,

Black person:
Nebula Being,
You match the first hue of infinity

Eta Ma'elo Uum

In one form mortal and, simultaneously, without
pattern,
You are the science,
You are the cosmic

Reject all logic or philosophy
that beats you into limitation

When we are young,

Crawling,
Before we have entered into the chrysalis,
We are beaten with
the contraction more crippling than labor pain
the spiked lynching rope of
"can't"
is wrapped around our necks,
snapping the bone,
disconnecting our mind/conscious from our
body/action,
denying us the chance to manifest the internal
gold,
like a curse to the soul,
a whip into membrane,
a cattle brand
We wear denial under the layers of our skin,
Tainting the magic of our melanin with dullness

And though black is the color of a business suit,
a judge's robe, a priest's vestment, a royal's cape,
an artist's garb,
Though black is the color of royalty for those who
wear it merely as an adornment,
for those of us who wear Black as Skin,
It is the head to toe mark of repudiation:
We wear "can't" as flesh
The stigmata of denial

But I charge you with this knowledge,
With this key to transformation:
Reject all logic or philosophy

That beats you into limit
For black is also the color of the fabric of space,
Nebula Being,
You are the All,
You are the Is,

Colorimetry,
Visual electromagnetic radiation,
Perceptual, wavelength,
The science:
Black, a color with no hue/absorbs all light/into itself

Relativity,
Quantum physics, Stellar, Astronomical,
The science:
Black Hole,
A spacetime region from which /nothing can escape/gravity more powerful than the stuff of existence/into which existence itself is absorbed

Black living body,
Celebrate your achromaticism,
You are the Receiver of Universal Energy
Black, you are the science of infinite absorbency

As Black absorbs all,
So must you pull it all into you,
Every knowledge, every canon,
Every writ, every axiom,
Every hue of human possibility

Pull it in and hold it,
Become what attunes the pitch of your spirit,
What aims the mark of your lifeline
hold it,
in your core,
Give birth to it,
Living and vibrant,

Descendent of mystics, healers, and medicine priests,
Child of Dambala

In one form mortal and, simultaneously, without pattern,
You are the science,
You are the cosmic

Black person:
Nebula Being,
You match the first hue of infinity

2013: When First I Rejoined My Old Tribe

XXXV. In-Formation (A'kamaulauah atamammah)

And now I have rejoined that world,
Which I left behind

Because I grew tired of being the only rebel,
And because other rebels were hard to find
And because I grew tired of being alone,
And because love was so distant,
And because bills needed to be paid,
And because being a rebel was expensive,
And because everyone said that my energy had changed,
And that I was welcome among the robots again,
And because opportunities had presented themselves,
And because I could type and create systems,
And because I could believe and hope,
And because I could take another's mission and in it find purpose,
And because I had begun to heal,
And because I had treated most of my wounds,
And because I live again and operate again and breath again,
And because I was normal again

Golden child to black sheep to golden child again

And because I enjoyed the adulation,
And the validation,
And the appreciation,

And because they told me I was great,
And because they told me I was welcome,
And because they told me I was gifted,
And needed,
And they even said I was beloved,
And because my ego needed feeding,
And because I had been alone for so long,
And because I had dealt with my pain and my suffering and because I had let it all go,
And because I had stood so long and had not fallen down and believed that I finally could walk again without falling,
And because I had moved past those obstacles,
And because I started taking the train to Michigan Avenue and to the Gold Coast to be around the wealthy people, and because their energy rubbed off on me and I could feel alive again and feel happy again and feel the opportunities for life again,
And because I could be around joyous people,
And because walking and traveling proved to me that the sickness I thought existed was relenting, and because I learned to be fearless again,
And because I regained my courage,
And because I stripped away all the hate and anger,
And because I learned that I was loved, if only by some,
And because I didn't need to be so defensive anymore,

And because I learned that not everyone wanted to hurt me,
And because I finally understood why I was always so angry,
And because I became happy by making the choice to be happy,
And because I became free by making the choice to be free,
And because I wanted to live again by accepting the beauty of life,
And so I began to walk forward and live again

Golden child to black sheep to golden child again

And because my friend called me with a job,
And because the job paid well,
And because it was easy to impress them,
And because it was easy to dress up again,
And because I looked good in dress clothes,
And because I impressed them with my svelte figure and tight shirts,
And because I was tall with a deep voice,
And because I spoke the King's English,
And because I pronounced all my t's and r's,
And because I was very smart,
And because I was good at nearly everything,
And because my gifts made space for me,
And because I got paid every two weeks,
And because I could take care of my skin and shave and bathe and wash my clothes again and be impressive, instead of the wild Afro and crazed

beard and unwashed skin and unwashed clothes
that came from depression,
And because some considered me handsome,
And because I could get the job done,
And because I impressed some people,
And because I began climbing the ranks,
And because the positions opened for me,
And because the church that once rejected me now
sat me on their pulpit,
And because the new leadership liked me,
And because the general leadership liked me,
And because they all saw me as a good trophy to
sit before the masses,
And because my ego needed feeding,
And because I liked to help people,
And because I loved to preach,
And because I wanted to save others from the
suffering I endured by sharing with them the ways
around the pits and valleys and obstacles,
And because I loved to help,
And because my father taught me to drive,
And because I had my first car,
And because it was a sports car,
And because I made everyone laugh,
And because I did my job,
And because my coworkers liked me,
And because my bosses liked me,
And because I went from a staff member to having
my own office, and because I could hold my own,
and because I had business cards and my own line,
and because I had multiple cell phones, and

because I could finally afford the $200 fragrance
and the $400 coat and the $800 outfit,
And because I began to shop down on fashion row
and on Michigan Avenue,
And because I looked like I fit in with the wealthy
people, even if I was still living in my bedroom at
home,
And because I began to impress everyone, and
because I gained new friends,
And because I loved my friends,
And because they loved me back,
And because I was on the ministerial staff,
And because I was the site coordinator,
And because I was the administrative coordinator,
And because I was back in the expedited Master's
Degree program,
And because my friends hung out almost daily,
And because I could travel out of state,
And because I had to travel out of state for work,
And because the paychecks increased,
And because I finally was one of them...

I jumped in,
Full believer

Golden child to black sheep to golden child again

I jumped in,
Full believer

Golden child to black sheep to golden child again

Yeah,
I jumped in,
Full believer,

Golden child to black sheep to golden child again

And they believed me,
Full believers

Golden child to black sheep to golden child again

And I believed them,
Full believer/Fool believer

Golden child to black sheep to golden child again

In formation
Reformation
Information
Reformation
In formation

XXXVI. Predominate (Ahtahmah'eh Ra'al'maht'ma'al)

Here I am,
Predominate,

I sleep with the bright ceiling light on each night,
No bed,
nothing but a hard boxspring that I lay atop,
the pain keeps me tense and locked in to the
performance, no relaxing, stay alert,
my laptop stays open in front of me,
playing reruns, because I can't sleep when it's too
quiet,
I fear silence because I can hear how large the
world is around me, and I need the world to be
small and within my grasp for this performance to
keep succeeding...

My bedroom has no furniture beside that
boxspring and a bookshelf, no television or chairs,
My name-brand and luxury-label clothes lay in
piles covering the floor,
I starch and iron them each morning until they
look new, I spend hundreds replacing them every
month,
The lady at my job told me I look like I'm straight
out of a fashion magazine,
If you look good, they'll think you're good and
they'll trust you and fear you and reward you,
And that feeds my ego and emptiness
After all, what else do I have?

My luxury toiletries and personal items are on the
top level of a bookshelf which is full of fantasy
novels that I no longer read and sheet music that I
no longer play,
because it's either the business life and
maintaining the illusion it demands
or it's imagination,
I choose the business life because it pays the bills...
imagination always reminds me that none of this
really matters,
and I don't want to be reminded of that,
I've jumped into this performance,
Full believer,
And I have anything else but this...

My expensive cologne in my work bag,
$220 a bottle,
I smell like nothing they've ever smelled before,
I wear so much they go home smelling like me,
I've learned that if you smell good,
it increases the positive way people receive you by
far, it doubles the way you captivate people,
you entrance them,
even more,
you mark your territory,

I still live in my parent's house,
in the bedroom I've had since I was a child,
But gone is the bedroom of my childhood,
I painted the walls dark,

And with the mess of clothes covering the floor,
the stripped boxspring, the broken bookshelf, the
bare walls, and the stench from the food and
garbage I often leave in the corner,
it seems more like the lair of a wild animal than
the living space of a human

I like it that way,
It doesn't feel like home, it's merely a stopping
place on my consistent journey forward,
The lack of comfort keeps me connected,
energized, and at watch,
I can't afford to slip, to disconnect, or to lose my
grip,
Do you know why?

Come...I'll tell you a secret that only I know...

This life...
this life that I have built...
deep down I know it is a palace balanced on a
obelisk...
the obelisk itself held up by a bubble...and I
know...
the slightest disturbance will pop the bubble and
topple the palace,
and undo the whole thing

But here I am,
Predominate,

I'm doing this for my family too,
They've had a depressed, broken, jobless
son/nephew for too long,
Look at me now,
I'm finally one of the good ones,
The people at the church have accepted me again,
The family thinks I'm accomplished,
I'm everything they've always wanted,
They're so proud,

...except that aunt who has hated me since I was a
child,
And who left the church our family goes too
because I was a part of the ministry and she was
tired of them mentioning me and seeing me on the
pulpit,
But she's been that way since I was a child, and
I've long-since learned to overlook her...

But I can't be around my family too long...
I leave the house at 6 AM each day,
I get home at 11 PM each night,
Most of that time is spent out exploring every
nook and cranny of the city,
Going to the movies and restaurants with my
friends,
Finding anything to avoid going back home,
Because even though I still live at home,
I hate it there and the people there will drain me if
I'm around them too long,

They'll remind me of the fear that I had beaten into submission,
They'll strip me of the courage that is now at an all-time high,
They'll make me remember the looming sense of doom I shot so far into the depths of the galaxy that it'll take millions of light-years to return,
They'll make me recall the resignation that has since been dispatched,
They'll summon again the disillusion I replaced with hope,
They'll reflect the brokenness I had fixed,
They'll make me forget the purpose and the hope for the future that I have returned to,

Do you know why?

Come...I'll tell you a secret that only I know...

This life...
this life that I have built...
deep down I know it is a palace balanced on a obelisk...
the obelisk itself held up by a bubble...and I know...
the slightest disturbance will pop the bubble and topple the palace,
and undo the whole thing

But here I am,
Predominate,

The brother of my friend came to me,
"You've changed. It's not the clothes or the job you have. It's you. Your energy is just on a new level"
His eyes were alight

Everybody believes this performance,
Even me...
I don't even realize it's an act anymore,
I'm beyond autopilot,
I am the character, I believe him, I live him, I am him...

It didn't start as an act,
I really wanted to live again,
To climb again,
To grow again,

But in a world where everything is fake and everything is image and everything is topical, it's hard not to become like them,

They're like capped teeth,
Rotting cavities under porcelain veneers,
And if you aren't careful,
You'll find yourself like them,
Under a shiny new veneer, unbrushed,
And you'll get cavities like theirs...
But at least the porcelain is beautiful...
That brilliant porcelain smile so full of shit,
No wonder they use porcelain for toilet bowls too

I have the nicest car of all my friends,
The nicest clothes of everyone I know,
Everywhere I go, I stand out,

Yet, when I cast the prescient eye forward,
There is a fog I cannot pierce,
I'm living in the now-moment,
I don't know what will become of this,
Because it's all just a performance

The job is so easy that it's a distraction,
The image that I've carefully built and crafted
feeds my ego,
If I don't have the compliments, then what else do
I have

Sometimes,
I drive down 95th street until my gas tank is near
empty and the buildings give way to massive
forests preserves,
And I play the saddest music ever,
And I park the car and sit there,
And I breathe as deeply as I can,
And sometimes I start to cry,

And how could I possibly be happy...

I've created a character who feeds all my
emptiness,
He is more than what people wanted of me,
He is what they all wish they could be,

And that's why they both love and hate him,

The performer in me loves playing him,
The storyteller in me loves crafting the specifics of him,
My ego loves the compliments he receives,

But I know, deep down, that he's an empty amusement,

And that's why I sleep in this messy bedroom,
It's like a cocoon,
Separate from the rest of the universe by its unusualness,
It is my dressing room, reflecting my psyche,
I can come out and be the butterfly, then return to my lair to rest for the next day's performance,
Deep down, as messy as this bedroom,

It's a wonderful role,
But I can't even afford an apartment because all my money goes into maintaining him,

And everyone's changed,
Anyone who's not my friend is threatened by my character,
Perhaps I've made him too haughty,
Too confident, too headstrong,

Don't they know he only walks with such a dismissive stride and speaks so strongly and keeps everyone at such a distance because he's so deeply afraid of connecting, of being hurt, of not being loved...

A few of the people resent me, are jealous of me, distrust me, when they used to be so kind...
When you join the fake society where people are accustomed to being fake,
They assume everyone is as false as they are,
Even those who come with authenticity are distrusted,
After all,
Who would be foolish enough to be real in this world

Don't they know...don't they remember...
The me who would never hurt them
The me who had been hurt,
Can't they see that my character could do everything but hurt them,
Can't they see that I might be playing a role,
But I'm playing it with all my heart and I mean it

And all my so-called friends,
They say to me,
"You're the best!"
Don't they see how deeply I'm hurting,
How empty this is,
How I don't know where this will go,
How I've built and constructed a life to live, yet,
I'm not truly living life,

I'm trapped, content but not happy,

Won't they run away with me,
To some wild hippy commune, some joyous new life, some great adventure,

Before the palace topples, the obelisk falls, the bubble bursts,

Do you know why?

Come...I'll tell you a secret that only I know...

This life...
this life that I have built...
deep down I know it is a palace balanced on a obelisk...
the obelisk itself held up by a bubble...and I know...
the slightest disturbance will pop the bubble and topple the palace,
and undo the whole thing

But here I am,
Predominate

XXXVII. Streetlights – A Song of Sadness (Ket'emll a'wao lt)

All I see are streetlights,
The sun hides behind the lightless blight of night,
Roads go on forever,
My car leads nowhere

I find I'm so lonely,
The bright blues have turned to yellows & gray,
All I know for sure is: I don't hold the cure,
and all that I know has changed,
And all I know is what they sold me,
And nothing
is the same

Streetlights come,
Their warm glow birthing the matter of night

I wish these streetlights would go away

All I see are streetlights,
The road goes on a long, taxed, & tired while
I have lost my whole Heart,
and I can't find my smile

I find I'm so lonely,
The whole world, an already lost game
I don't know my journey,
and nothing's the same

Streetlights come,
Their warm glow birthing the matter of night

I wish these streetlights would go away

All I need is clear blue day,
I wish these streetlights would go away

XXXVIII. More Than This - A Song of Longing
(A'tukuwo'ua'ah'ulaul Mmah'tah'to'weh'l)

Every day I woke up,
I know we've built the whole world all wrong,
At the core of what I'm living for,
I know we've lost the meaning of the song
And one day, one day, one day,
One day,
We'll go somewhere far from here,
Somewhere past all our fear,
One day we'll go somewhere where there's more
than this

Because what are we searching for,
And what do we hope to find,
And where is the open door,
And what is the higher sign,

All I know,

Is I want something more than this...

2016: When First I Realized A Thing Had Been Broken Again

XXXIX. Pastel and Shell (Eck Hu'wotm Ki'amo'go)

Cerulean-Azure sky,
One of those days where the sun and moon are out
at the same time
Cosmic feng-shui,
In the western sky:
*An elemental ball shining through the ozone, nuclear-yellow,
blinding on an angle*
To the east:
*Half a moon like a white brush stroke on a transparent
indigo canvas*
A flaming sphere burning through the atmosphere
An alabaster-bone sea sponge in sweet blue water

It was one of those days and I
Was so riddled by despair and ache that
I wanted to jump out of the car as it was moving,
And run as far as my legs would go,
To somewhere where all I had to do was love and
hibernate

For you, I carved a world with a broken
hand...until you broke me whole

I'm back there again, broken from being a
champion,
The boy that no one loved,
The years I spent training like a method actor to

Become the man that everyone admired,
But it means nothing,
Like ashes on a forehead, they marked me inferior,
When I was still young enough to receive it into the grain of my being,
now I give everything, even health and sanity, for those moments of validation,
Am I finally good enough to be loved?

I always find heroes who are just like me,
I forget they're only human, and like me, broken,
They use me as pawns for their battle to be great,
And leave me shattered,
Halfway between, the spirit world always opens when they break me,

I used to hold you as my everything,
And so I built my castles in your lands,
But you proved to me your inadequacies,
With this, how will my castles stand?
Give me a statement of intent,
Because I don't want to be hurt again,
I gave my consciousness to your missions,
my heartbeat to your war,
I was your banner-holder,
And you left me used, crushed and crumbled,
By the weight of being your champion,
And now I'm broken,
Halfway between, the spirit world opens,

Dulled and disconnected, the parted veil leaves me stunned,

Years ago, I'd spend my last dollars to get the bus to the suburbs,
I'd ride two hours just to be your servant, you abandoned me under love's guise,
That day, I looked west out the window,
The sky turned green and the sun was bright red,
I had an apocalypse-vision in that moment, the end of creation,
A profound breaking in the veil, a cross between the worlds,
Across from the strip mall, the bank, and the coffee-house,
Lost in higher sight, as the bus rolled along:
The first time I was broken being a champion for her, she drove me mad,
Halfway between, the spirit world always opens when they break me

Years ago, at night, walking in the parking lot,
Of a place I only visited to fulfill their desires, just a pawn for their validation,
At the city's edge, full view of the western horizon, no buildings to block the star-lit heavens,
The moon was setting to the west,
So low on the horizon it looked vast and gigantic,
Unearthly and frightening,

It scared me through and through,
On the bus ride home,
I wrote a prophesy for that moon:
The second time I was broken being a champion
for them, they drove me mad,
Halfway between, the spirit world always opens
when they break me

Greece, Moscow, and Cairo on my television
screen,
Me in the dark room watching,
Comedies and action films during the night,
It's all I can watch, nothing too deep, else it will
shatter the veil,
Which keeps me disconnected from the real,
The stimuli which will overwhelm me when I'm in
these spaces

Halfway between, pastel and shell, blue and white,
Atmosphere to ozone to gravity to crust to mantle
to core,
Soul, consciousness, carnal. Planet, star, and
galaxy.
It's all as alive as we are,
And I'm halfway between,
The spirit world always opens when they break
me,
And I wonder this time,
Can I fix it?

One of those days when the moon and sun were
out at the same time
Pastel and shell
Cosmic feng-shui
Will it repair the chaos?

The castles I built in their lands have crumbled,
My friends whisper that it's a good thing,
I can finally be my own champion,
But me,
I just want to be happy again,
by all means,
happy again

XL. To Witness Totality (Ka'haroum Pa'Net Huam'l)

Everything in this house is broken...
but you can't beat a wound into healing
folie à deux, shared madness,
the sad aunt or schizophrenia,
Disassociation

It is said that when you feel disconnected from your self,
when you no longer know who you are,
when life is vastly different from what it was,
it is to be considered a medical condition

I call it,
The veil being broken

This world as we know it is but bodies crashing in
the void, with no aim,

(Ag-Ot Sikag Bui Pl)

Gasoline rainbows in puddles on the street
Victims of circumstance and the illusion of fate-
time,
and lightning in a bottle,
Clown makeup to hide suffering,
Lovers,
Revolution is not a genre,
The generic quality of it all,
The sadness of jazz,
Driving down 95th into the sunset,

Successfully overcoming the cellular suffering
inherited from our forespirits in Pangea (siwolau'
pamwma)

Rock woman, anime, vibe,
energy, consumption, love
Hip hop,
golden brown,
future, energy, human to technology

I've known the pain locked in black,
I've seen the raconteur who eats of black bodies
(Koma'kiloret Amnu)

I remember oranges and coffee at the living room
table,
The house with the white picket fence

It's come to introversion,
being alone, needing space,
hoping to find someone whose alone shit matches
my alone shit.

Wandering & the latitudes of solitudes

I've begged for light healing,
But what they made me give to the midnight sun
was never holy,

All I know is I can't go back alone

That is, I can't go back
to being
alone
...not with the way they have marked me
(Sibulo'ahuwuah)
The farm store on the road,

Illinois,
Two hours outside Chicago,
On the road to Galena,

Past the picturesque hills with unbothered cows,
The processing plants

A brick and wooden shack,
A mom and daughter in chairs on the porch,
They sold pumpkins, potatoes, and squash,
Cabbage, onions, green beans, and eggplant,
Tiny colorful figurines,
Handmade homemade toys,
wallets
and wind chimes

My eyes were glued to that shack,
I almost drove off the road,
If I had my way, I would've pulled over and lived
there with them,
Selling vegetables and knick-knacks
Use all that business acumen I'd gained for
something truly good,

Sign them up so they could accept credit cards
from travelers
And help them cover their products in the rain

I left my soul in that shack,
I didn't pull over,
I didn't enter it,
But it entered me

There,
I witnessed totality

XLI. The Merkabah of Modernity (Et' Umlah Amah)

Quasars and the Souls of the Dead which have
rejoined the universe
compose a rispetto for those born,
the cradle essence of the lives yet to be,

Light: a marked point

Color this hymn in sweetness,

Sage spirit, brown sand heart,
Roaming body,
matted hair in wind,
sphere seed,
magnetic,
The high place where the concept of civilization
ends,
Meditating,
balanced on the light,
firefly,
Soil dancer,
Apple and wooden bowl,
Soup and topaz,
circle and energy

I mark my soul with changing shades of light,
My person draws a line through the wind as I
move
over the landscape, eating the meta blue of sky
born in the light of dusk, but not the sun itself,

I am healed when I disconnect,
Red tree, gold flower, blue god, tan owl,
When I hold my ear to solitude,
Leaving society,
In a circle, a being-chariot,
Letting it carry me to the edge and nowhere of today,
Carried to the silent, unmoving wheel of noontime,
when I reconnect to sweetly tolling bell of clearness,

When I, gripping the steering wheel, drive, windows down,
music loud enough to bless pedestrians with the tonal vibration
of each instrument,
driving,
Until the concrete buildings and paved streets yield their authority,
to the oxygen of trees, and sign,

I accept an empty lot, a corner store, a porch,
a cookout, an expressway, a friend's room, a forest preserve
as my temple

I worship catharsis in any space that accepts my release,
I heal wherever creation offers me sustenance,

The macro, the cosmic, the chamber and source of nature,
The womb within the silent fabric of totality

When I realize I don't have to conquer any world,
Except the racing heartbeat of consciousness,

This is the merkabah of modernity

2018: When First I Walked The New Orbit

XLII. The Long-Haul of Survival (Ma'ashl m'ahluwal'ah puwo'ah)

Scientists ponder how humankind will survive all
the things that threaten us in the near future and
the far future to come,

The biological,
The technological,
The natural,
The extraterrestrial,
The results of our central human nature,

Theologians and scholars wonder too,
Thinkers and philosophers,
Shaman and teachers,
Workers and parents,
Idealistic youth,
Disillusioned youth,
Everyone who has been touched by the intimate
realization that we are finite beings on a rock in a
universe that renders us infinitely infinitesimal by
the fact of its vastness

How do we live in the face of chaos uncertainty,
points of human insanity, and universal instability,

I have discovered the way,
I wish that it would wrap you in mystery,
And bedeck you with wander,
But the answer is like breathing,

I learned it from every wise and beautifully
wizened old person who has, with the simplicity
that can only be gained through survival,
Shared the very secret to survival

As toddlers, we learn
To balance on our legs,
To put one foot in front of the other
To transfer our weight from foot to foot and from
leg to leg,
And there move our whole self forward,

We do this until it becomes as natural as
breathing,

And that is how we survive,

Eminent danger?
A wild animal?
A violent human?
Dangerous circumstances?
An act of nature?
As quickly as possible,
place one foot in front of the other and move the
whole self forward until the human vessel in
which you reside is no longer at risk

It's how we secure opportunities,
an interview?
the job we have?
new places, things,

people and sights?
Place one foot in front of the other and move the
whole self forward until you are where you need to
be to progress

It's how we prevent those we love from leaving us,
In an argument,
In a separation,
When the truths needed to reignite love have not
been spoken,
Place one foot in front of the other and move the
whole self forward until you have caught up with
the person who has fooled themselves into
believing that leaving is the option,
And tell the truth that reverberates the core of
your Self,
Until they understand and until they are marked
by the intimate utmosts of your being

It's how we survive when we are relearning life,
When we don't know what the future holds,
When we suddenly need pills to survive,
When we feel like we can't go on,
When we don't want to go on,
When we feel as if we're losing touch with reality,
When we hate those we once loved,
When they hate us too,
When we've lost everything,
When we still have much but it feels as though
we've lost it all,

When we lose people and don't know how to adjust,
When we suffer,
When we cry but no one is there to hear it and console us,
When we cry and there are people near,
but they don't know how to heal or console us,
When we cry and the people near us don't want to hear or console us,
When we can't see past tomorrow,
When succeeding or arriving feels like it's too far away,
When we begin to age and feel as if there's so much to do and time is moving so quickly,
When we feel we are now enough,
When we are enough but it's still not enough,
When we realize we are not infinite,
When we realize that we won't be everything we want to be,
When we realize that life isn't always fair or kind but it's always equal, one way or another,

Place one foot in front of the other and move the whole self forward,
Until tomorrow comes,
And the tomorrow next,
And the tomorrow next,
And the tomorrow next,
And on...

XLIII. I Name Myself (Umatahmolo L'Yuehamolo)

In some cultures,
A child is given a temporary name,
Until they reach an age where they can define who they are,
And choose a new name,

And whether that name encapsulates who they truly are or who they wish to be,
It is good,

For even those who created us and bore us cannot know the fullness of us,

Even when we are in the womb,
Our minds create thoughts our mothers will never know and our fathers never could,
And the complexity of those thoughts increase as we age,

And therefore, no one but we can ever truly knew the depths of us,
No one but we can ever live in our individual flesh, and feel what it is to be our individual selves,
No one but we will ever know all that there is to know as completely as it can be comprehended by our minds

And so I, therefore, challenge the idea
That anyone but I can name I,

That anyone but me can know me
And so,
I name myself,

I chose the sounds that will define me,
The phonetic utterances that will represent me,
The letters that will indicate me

I stand before the I Am and the Is,
The Universe and the Us,
The We

And I redeclare who I am

Because it is the only way that I can go forward,

For if everything in a package has changed,
The label must change to reflect it,

I am no captive,
I am no owned thing,
I am no pet, no slave, no servant,

I name myself,
Because it is the only way I can become

XLIV. The New Orbit (Eh'to oh'lahw'h Mah'la)

A planet in orbit will revolve forever and can never be free of the object which keeps it

If I wish to be new, to transform, to be free, and to expand my life to new experiences and new lands and new beings, then my orbit must change

I have attempted to get closer to my star and to get further away,
But it's still the same star,
With the same nature,
The same people,
the same patterns,
the same stigma,
the same lifestyle,
the same choices,
the same sameness,

And so I finally went in search of the star that had always matched my composition,

And I have found it

It was hard,
And some of me was broken off, never to be recovered in escaping the gravity of the old star,

But the new star whispered to me,

"What you are now is what you were always meant to be, what you lost was never you"

And my new star, and my new orbit around it, encourages me,

The period of acclimation will not be easy

My atmosphere must adjust to the new particles and flares and gamma rays and X-rays,
My oceans must adjust to the new sun's effects on its tides,
My terrestrial construction must adjust to the new gravitational force,
My crops must adjust to the new lightning and the new heat,
My planet must familiarize itself with the vistas of its new orbit,

But with that old star, I was approaching an event horizon,

And now, I am in natural revolution,
In the life-zone,

And my Earth will be well,

Someday, I know

This is the New Orbit

Dedications

I offer thanks and gratitude to all the people who have shared the journey with me thus far. The contributions, lessons, love, pain, joy, sorrow, and energy which they have brought to my life inspired this collection.

In loving memory of Nancy Ann Kurtz and Willis Ware

Author's Message

This collection covers many points of my life. The uncertain, angry, disillusioned, focused teenaged years full of art, music, prophesy, exploration, and the newness of experiencing love, balanced by a profound and gaping brokenness, disconnection from the world around me, and unrecognized toxicity as the norm. The breakdown in my late teenage years marked by depression, causing me to retreat into a cocoon which inevitably became a wilderness space for growth; the pilgrimage of learning, discovery, and healing that followed. The phoenix years of my early to mid 20's full of drive, energy, confidence: the successful rat race. The second breakdown in my late 20s that revealed to me that the life I had built was ersatz; that I was an artist and that I had to live what I was born to be and in the way my mind could healthily experience life. My early 30s, adjusting to the new normal of living with clinical anxiety and depression, abandoning a previously successful professional life. embarking on a new professional journey as an artist and walking the path I always should have, redefining relationships, and attempting to find level ground, happiness, and contentment again. Thus far, my life has been equal parts desert and garden, carved-out emptiness and unparalleled fulfillment. I hope that this collection contains something which may inspire you. I, too, have walked those roads which you walk. It is possible and your journey is not alone. We are in this together. We are still walking forward. We will live in fullness and allow ourselves to be fully what we are meant to be.

-Yelayu

Review

Erstwhile Orbits & Newformed Spheres is a collection of autobiographical poems composed by Umohowet Yelayu. Chronological and ordered by periods of life, it begins with youthful poems of ardent first-love and discovery. Before long, there is a shift to airy philosophy and the heavy esoteric, as life lessons and experiences slowly remove the rose-colored lenses. Emotional breakdowns and regroupings overtake the focus, leading to a renewed and blazing confidence, even if fault lines still rumble. Then, a diagnosis of mental illness followed by the desire for authenticity and true healing change the course of things once more. Here are powerful relationships as well as the deconstruction of those bonds; the development of strong religious beliefs and the painful losses of faith; transcendental philosophical brushstrokes and metaphysical pondering; declarations of personal strength and expressions of profound weakness. There is fragility & fortitude. Vulnerability, fear, anguish, melancholy, and misery. Power, courage, vigor, contentment. The result is a wholly human portrait.

"Pastel and Shell" discusses the dangers of giving oneself to others without reciprocity and "Your Palace In My Earth" expresses blind headfirst love. "The Prophet's Spice Truck" details a quasi-obsessive one-way-street friendship, while "Chinatown" paints the hopelessness of disillusioned youth. "Self-Righteous" sees an almost manic pride devolve into fetal desperation, as "The Naked God" is a request from a disciple begging to see a clearer sign of his Lord. "For Certain" is the doubt about everything that we all have in our quietest moments, and "Kinetic Slavery: Love As Religion" is a wild,

Mephistophelean piece about the depths of depression. "Suihallawuiyou (or the Girl at Ota'lu'kume)", is an art piece that uses the Delphic, the mystical, and the arcane to weave an experience. "To Witness Totality" and "The Merkabah of Modernity" express the search for healing, wholeness, and freedom. The closing pieces are almost matter-of-fact in their commitment to finding joy, fullness, and alignment with purpose.

These are pieces to be digested and, at the end of the collection, you will gain an insight into another's experiences which will reflect back to your own. This is no attempt at braggadocio, nor is it a pity-fest. It is an expression of the wholeness of life."

All poetry, photography, and images, including the book cover are copyrighted. Unauthorized reproduction is prohibited and is punishable by law. Text & Images Copyright © Umohowet Yelayu
All Rights Reserved

www.ingramcontent.com/pod-product-compliance
Lightning Source LLC
Chambersburg PA
CBHW031442040426
42444CB00007B/928